Dreamer in the Fields

My Life as a Child
Migrant Farm Worker

By John Hill

Vision
PUBLISHING
Carson, California

Unless otherwise indicated, all Scripture references are taken from the King James Version of the Holy Bible.

Dreamer in the Fields
My Life as a Child Migrant Farm Worker
ISBN 10: 0-9762730-7-1
ISBN 13: 978-0-9762730-7-3

Copyright © 2010
By John Hill

Published by:
Vision Publishing
P.O. Box 11166
Carson, California 90749-1166
Email: visionpub@sbcglobal.net
Phone: 310-537-0791

Publisher's Cataloging-in-Publication
(Provided by Quality Books, Inc.)

    Hill, John, 1945 Mar. 29-
       Dreamer in the fields : my life as a child migrant
    farm worker / by John Hill.
       p. cm.
       Includes bibliographical references.
       ISBN-13: 978-0-9762730-7-3
       ISBN-10: 0-9762730-7-1

       1. Hill, John, 1945 Mar. 29- 2. Child migrant
    agricultural laborers--United States--Biography.
    3. Dysfunctional families--Biography. 4. Migrant
    agricultural laborers--United States--Biography.
    5. Migrant agricultural laborers--Social conditions--
    Biography.   I. Title.

    HD1525.H55 2010   331.5'44'0973
                         QBI10-600065

TABLE OF CONTENTS

My grace is sufficient for thee: for my strength is made perfect in weakness.

—2 Corinthians 12:9

PREFACE

Author John Hill provides a penetrating glimpse into the life of child laborers during the 1950s in California's enormously productive Central Valley. It is a life that most city-dwellers hardly knew existed, yet these same fields were harvested more than 100 years ago by the Chinese and the Japanese when they picked the fruit orchards and worked beet fields. These early migrants would be followed by thousands of Filipinos and Mexicans. During the Depression, whites from such states as Oklahoma, Missouri, Arkansas, and Texas, forced off the land by greedy banks and gritty dust storms, came west to ply a living in these same fields. All endured great privation and maltreatment, but each generation conquered and moved on to a better existence.

There is every reason to believe that Hill's life story is typical of what the children of most migrant workers had to endure—hard labor, lack of proper schooling, inadequate nutrition, unsanitary living conditions, uncertain habitation, and so many other problems. What made Hill's childhood different was not only the fact that his family was black, but his parents were alcoholics, and he and his siblings were continual victims of a sort of benign parental neglect. Through it all, Hill kept questioning why life couldn't be better, even for a black family.

As one of ten children born to parents who were clearly victims of broken dreams and unrealized ambitions, young Hill kept his focus on what life could be rather than on what it actually was. He longed for a stable home with sober parents, regular meals, and a chance to get an education.

Even in conditions of dire poverty there can be good times, and the Hill family had some in spurts. The family was not without love, but the disease of alcoholism and its attendant conflicts easily trumped what could have otherwise been a fairly normal existence, even as they moved continually from one labor camp to another.

Still, young Hill kept the faith, believing all the while that God had a better plan for his life. In fact, God did. When the opportunity came, the nine-year-old seized it and held on to it with all that was in him.

Hill's autobiography, *Dreamer in the Fields*, adds to an important though little-known phase of black history.

—THE EDITORS

ACKNOWLEDGMENTS

Beginning with God, I give many thanks to those who always inspired me—Mom and Pop, the County of Fresno, my social workers, my teachers from grammar school through high school, and the many souls who always believed in me at Pop's church, Trinity Church of God in Christ in Fresno. I am so blessed that our paths crossed.

I also thank my wife, Mattie, and our four daughters—Natalie, Diona, Angela, and Anna—for their constant love, respect, and the pride they have shown in me. Without their affections, the work before you, like the author, would never have been completed.

DEDICATION

To Mom and Pop Seals, I will cherish your memory always.

1

MAN OF MYSTERY

I was born in the high-desert town of Hawthorne, Nevada, on March 29, 1945. Nestled between the gambling meccas of Reno and Las Vegas, it became the site of the Hawthorne Army Depot, the largest ammunition storage facility of its kind in the world. My father and mother, and my maternal grandfather and grandmother were working at the depot when I was born. A few months later, with the war ending, that all changed. Most of the blacks lost their jobs and, like my parents, would end up as migrant farm workers in California's Central Valley.

Every now and then my father would find better employment. He worked as a cook at the Camp Roberts Army base near San Miguel and as a garbage collector in Paso Robles. Most of the time, though, our lives were very difficult and uncertain, as we endeavored to survive as migrant laborers in such undistinguished California towns as Fairmead, Los Banos, and Riverdale. In fact, from 1945 to 1951, we spent most of our lives eking out a living in these three dusty towns.

I don't know much about my father—only about eight year's worth—and what I do know is still shrouded in secrecy. It is my belief that he was born either in Louisiana and moved to South Carolina, or he was born in South Carolina and moved to Louisiana. None of his ten children ever really knew for sure. Dad eventually left the South, and ended up in Los Angeles in the 1930s.

It has been suggested that he left home at the age of nine and joined the Ringling Brothers Barnum & Bailey Circus as a roustabout. We do have evidence that he was familiar with the circus. My oldest brother, Thomas, said once when the circus came to Paso Robles, Dad took him and introduced him to some of the workers by name. When I came along years later, I remember that any time the circus came to town, Dad would take us kids to see it.

After his death, we learned that Thomas Rory Hill was not his real name, which meant, among other things, that all but one of his children carried a bogus surname. My father's true name was Thomas William Smith.

My father died in March, 1970. In 1997, my sisters and I dug up records that indicated that the Dora he claimed as his sister who lived in South Carolina was actually his mother who lived in Los Angeles. Rumor has it that he changed his name because he was wanted by the police for some offense that he and my mother's stepfather committed while they were living in Los Angeles. But nothing so far has satisfactorily explained all the mystery concerning my father's past. So well covered were his tracks that we never met any of our relatives on my father's side, including our paternal grandparents, so we have never found out the whole story.

What made me and my siblings question my father's past even more was that Thomas, the eldest brother, bore the last name of Smith. From our research into piecing together his life, we discovered that Dad's father was a dark-skinned man from Alabama and his mother was a "high-yeller" Creole from Louisiana. At some point during his youth his parents divorced, and his mother remarried, this time to a man from France. Shortly afterward, the couple moved to Los Angeles, with Thomas, my dad, in tow.

In an effort to understand why Dad was so close-mouthed about his background, we speculated that his light-skinned Creole mother might have taken heat from her family for marrying a dark-skinned man from Alabama. Some segments of the black population in those days were so color-conscious that choosing a dark-skinned mate would have provoked the family to disown a daughter or son and any offspring from their union.

Dad was born in 1909. He stood about five feet, eleven inches tall and weighed roughly 200 pounds. He was brown-skinned, with curly hair, and he bore a slight resemblance to the great bebop-era bandleader and balladeer, Billy Eckstine. Oddly enough, he could sing like Eckstine, too. And that fine singing voice was a gift he passed on to my brothers and me.

A lot of things conspired to bring my parents to the labor camps of the 1950s: their lack of education, the absence of any marketable skills other than singing and dancing, the color of their skin, as well as the loss of their jobs at the Hawthorne Army Depot. Dad's schooling only extended as far as the third grade, while Momma got as far as the eighth. Their opportunities for success by any other measure proved elusive, so they did the best they could with what they had.

I was always impressed with Dad's abilities. To me he was a very smart man. He could read and write adequately enough, though his penmanship was barely legible, and he liked doing crossword puzzles. He also spoke some French, a gift from both his Creole mother and his French step-dad. Beyond that, he had an uncanny way of figuring almost any difficult problem out. He was once hired as a farm contractor in Riverdale because he was somehow able to estimate the amount of water needed to irrigate the farm's crops.

Dad never seemed to be at a loss as to how to get control of any given situation. Part of my father's great survival instinct was his sense of humor, which I admired greatly. He was always laughing, and he rarely took himself seriously. Generally speaking, you only got on his bad side by messing with his children. People, whether white, black, or brown, seemed to gravitate toward him. It didn't matter. Dad could communicate with farmers as well as with drunks on the streets. He had a way about him that drew people to him.

I also inherited his work ethic, though on numerous occasions he questioned whether that was true. My father was a hard-working man who showed up on time with one purpose in mind—to get the job done. For the time that he was in my life, I cherished being around him. He was a loving father, and he was fun-loving and great with us kids. He would joke with us and sing to us. He believed more in talking sternly than in physical discipline, but at times he would also employ the leather, especially on Thomas. The two of them never seemed to see things the same way, and Thomas was constantly leaving us to live with our grandmother in Fairmead. I don't ever remember him disciplining me physically, but I do remember going with him for rides and long talks when I was just eight years old.

"What are you going to be when you grow up, son?" he would ask.

"I don't know, Dad, but I want to go to school and get an education."

"Okay, that's good. Getting an education is good."

"And, Dad, I don't want to continue working in the fields."

"I can see that. You would starve to death if you tried to make a living working in the fields."

Dad would always tell me I was smart, and I believe he convinced me that I was. Even at that young age, my father saw something in me that to this day I sometimes struggle to see in myself.

When I was just eight, he would sometimes ask me to take care of the bills for the family.

"How much money did we make today, Little Curly?" he would ask.

"Oh, we made thirty dollars," I would reply.

"That's good, son."

I have no idea why he leaned on me so, but he would always turn to me for certain answers, as if he had blind faith in my eight-year-old judgment. He consistently reiterated the idea that I was going to make something of my life. "You are going to be something," he would say, convinced that I would somehow escape the drudgery of the labor camps. Much later, after leaving the Air Force, I drove to Santa Rosa to see him. It had been years since we had parted. He was living there with his second wife, Rosie. After a long visit he said it again: "Your mother and I knew you were going to be different than the rest of your brothers and sisters. There was something about you that was just different."

Concerning me, Dad was right more times than he was wrong.

2

MOMMA'S MISERY

My mother was born Alberta Gentry in Tulsa, Oklahoma, and was living there during the 1921 riot in the area they called Black Wall Street. It is considered by many to be the worst race riot in American history. Black Wall Street was in the thriving black section of Tulsa called Greenwood, which was separated by railroad tracks from the city's main commercial district. At the southern end of Greenwood Avenue, the main street running through Greenwood consisted of several blocks of red two- and three-story buildings that housed such black-owned businesses as newspapers, clothing and jewelry stores, grocery stores, butcher shops, dry goods stores, upholstery shops, barber and beauty salons and the like.

For its size of about 10,000 citizens, Greenwood had more than its share of prosperous entrepreneurs, including doctors, lawyers, bankers, and other professional people. In fact, that's how it came to be known as Black Wall Street. It had fine neighborhoods with large homes, though like any other city, it also had the ubiquitous poor that Jesus said we would always have with us. A great number of whites—and blacks—had been drawn to the areas around Tulsa by the oil boom of the early 1900s. Blacks streamed in from Arkansas, Missouri, Mississippi, and other parts of the South.

Momma was about nine or ten years old when a white mob gathered outside the Tulsa courthouse with the intention of lynching a nineteen-year-old black man who was accused of the attempted rape of a seventeen-year-old white female elevator operator. As the mob grew more insistent and unruly, a number of Greenwood's black male citizens who were concerned about the accused man's safety, gathered in an effort to ensure that there would be no lynching. It's reported that they met with the sheriff to offer their services but were turned down.

However, a race riot ensued when the small group of armed blacks confronted the mob. Several shots were fired from each side, leaving several whites and blacks either wounded or dead. With that, both sides retrenched. The blacks jumped into their cars and fled to Greenwood, and the whites then went on a killing and burning spree. Armed groups charged through Greenwood, beating and shooting blacks, and looting their homes and businesses before torching them. Stores, office buildings, banks, restaurants, hotels, two hospitals, and a library were consumed by flames. Some blacks fled to safety in the woods or to neighboring towns, while others stayed to defend their homes and businesses.

The blacks were heavily outmanned and outgunned by the white majority, whose numbers included a well-armed National Guard unit and a number of law-enforcement personnel. Blacks were reportedly gunned down from the air as well as from the ground. The captured were put into makeshift internment centers around the city, and Tulsa quickly enacted a law that Greenwood could not be rebuilt. Although the Oklahoma Supreme Court later overturned the law, the damage had been done. What was once a promising showcase for black enterprise was wiped off the map in a matter of about sixteen hours.

Momma told us that she and her mother, whose name was Sarah Miller, along with a number of other blacks, were running to escape the bedlam when several whites began chasing them. Thinking they might be beaten or killed, they picked up the pace. But they soon realized that the white group was on a different mission. They were actually begging the blacks to stay. Such were the peculiarities of Southern life. After all, blacks provided almost all the domestic labor and in some cases had nursed and nurtured the very whites who were screaming racial epithets, beating and shooting blacks, and looting their homes and businesses. In some cases, these blacks were even considered to be members of their families.

With their hopes of economic freedom burned to the ground, many blacks left Tulsa for good. My mother, her brother, and mother moved west to Los Angeles.

My mother was an attractive, brown-skinned woman, who stood about five feet, three inches tall and weighed about 140 pounds. She had somewhat short hair that she always kept neatly pressed. Momma often talked about her family, but never about Dad's. We knew both her parents and grandparents, but she was probably as much in the dark about Dad's side of the family as we were since she never mentioned them.

I believe she and my father got together in the early thirties in a club or dance hall in Los Angeles where he was a singer and she was a dancer. I'm still not sure if they ever married, but I suspect they did. Again, the information about their early years is sketchy, but we learned much of what we do know from a fairly reliable source, Momma's best friend, Madonna, who also was my godmother. Madonna claimed she was the one who introduced them to each other.

Momma taught us all the dances of the twenties and thirties—the jitterbug, the Charleston, the Lindy Hop...

...and the black bottom, a dance which proved to be somehow prophetic.

3

LIQUOR WAS KING

There is no question that my parents loved one another. After having ten children together, one might think there would be no question of it, but that is not always the case with large families. My parents were frequently lovey-dovey, hugging and kissing, and saying sweet things to one another. And they always expressed that love to us children.

But there was indeed a dark side to their lives, and it would be far more correct to say that they were lovey-dovey only as long as they were sober. Under the influence of alcohol, however, which they often were, these two normally even-tempered and delightful people changed their personalities, becoming argumentative, aggressive, and pugilistic. Suddenly, they were like two street-fighters who brawled openly and would use any object they could find as a weapon to hurt one another.

My parents' battles were thoroughly upsetting to me. My siblings and I would take bets on who was going to win, but when it was all over we'd go outside to sit and cry. We were all losers, and I think that thought alone may have been the most devastating part of my young life.

I believe Momma wanted to keep the family together, but the marriage was destined to unravel because the drinking, fighting, and the abuse by my father ultimately became

11

just too much to bear. At some point she got tired of being both a migrant worker and an abused wife, which was an extremely difficult combination, especially when coupled with raising nine children. She would tell me much later that she left because she wanted some stability in her life. I believe the pressures and the longing for a better life pushed her to the edge. The time came when it got to the point that she could not handle it anymore.

My mother was a good woman and a good mother. She watched over us as a hen watches over her brood. Even though we had little or no money for clothing and shoes, Momma saw that we were always clean and neatly dressed. She washed our clothes by hand and ironed them with a heavy iron that was heated on old wood-burning stoves. She was very diligent and careful about the way we looked. She neatly combed and brushed the boys' hair and plaited the girls' hair. She didn't allow us to go around dirty, though we were dirt poor. We had to take baths regularly, whether in a river, a canal, or in the famous No. 3 galvanized tub that was so prevalent in homes that lacked inside plumbing. She made sure we had food to eat. Of course, none of these things held true when she was drinking; then she did not care what we did or how we looked.

Still, they were remarkable parents when they were sober, and I never saw them argue at such times. I wished they could have seen what drinking was doing to their lives and the lives of their nine surviving children, who loved and needed them. We were a good family, but drinking controlled us and caused Momma and Dad to try to outdo each other. Whatever Dad did, Momma did. If he was out running the streets, she went out and ran the streets, too. If he wanted to drink himself into a stupor, she wanted to do it, too. She wasn't the type of woman who could put up with being left with the kids while he was out. No matter what, she was going to be out there doing what he did.

I felt she should have been there for us kids in spite of what Dad did. I had a hard time understanding her actions. I felt mothers shouldn't ever leave their children.

My mother was nobody's pushover. She had a mean streak in her that might have been honed by her frequent combats with Dad. On one occasion Momma and another woman got into an argument that apparently had something to do with Dad, who was known for his dalliances. Momma was outside making lye soap at the time, so it clearly was not the best time for anyone to pick a fight with her. Throughout rural America, lye was a popular and inexpensive alkali for making a coarse, all-purpose household soap. The lye crystals were mixed with water in order to liquefy them before being combined with hot cooking grease. The mixture was then allowed to set as the soap was formed. Anyone familiar with lye knows that it is a very caustic substance that can cause severe burns if it comes in contact with flesh, especially as a liquid.

When Momma went into the house, apparently to mix the lye crystals with hot water, the woman followed her to the door, in spite of repeated warnings to leave her alone. In a blink, Momma doused her with the hot liquid and the woman took off running and screaming. She must have suffered serious burns, because a short time later Dad took us to visit Momma in jail in the town of Madera.

Both of my parents at one time had dreams of succeeding in the entertainment business, but neither of them made it. All their legitimate dreams became secondary to their exploitation of liquor and everything that was illegitimate. It was as if they felt that the laws did not apply to them. Under today's rules of the road, Dad would have probably spent more time behind bars than behind the wheel for driving drunk, and of course, there were child-labor laws that were constantly violated. And it was nothing for Dad to stop the car if he spotted a wino walking uncertainly or simply sleeping off the effects of cheap booze. Under his direction, we would help him rifle the pockets of these drunks and take anything they had of value.

Such was the sad state of our morality, but I do not believe my parents did anything different from what others might have done, given the same set of circumstances. When compared to those in similar straits, I'm sure their activities would not seem outrageous or strange. People do what they think they have to do to survive.

I would like to believe they tried for as long as they could to take care of each other and their children. But ultimately, they failed both us and one another.

4

THE KIDS

My earliest childhood memory, I think, was of a time when I was around three or four years old. We lived in the little town of Los Banos. My sister Laura, who was about three years older, was having a birthday party and she wanted me out of the way. She called Momma and told her to remove me from the room. Her words hurt me, so I flattened her birthday cake by sitting on it. I can't remember if my mother spanked me or just laughed. I suspect the latter. As we got older, Laura would become my closest sister and confidante.

I don't know if the fact that all my brothers and sisters were born in California while I was born in Nevada contributed to my feelings of being different, or somehow separate, but I always felt I was different from my siblings. I loved my brothers and sisters, and I constantly strove to abolish any idea that I was not just another Hill child, as they were, but the feeling was there nonetheless. It was not a need for my siblings' acceptance that fueled my drive for a life beyond the labor camps, but a determination not to follow in my parents' footsteps. I knew there was something different, and I wanted whatever that difference was.

There were ten of us, all born within a twelve-year period, but one died early. Thomas was born in 1938; Glenn

Arthur, whom we called Baby Brother, in 1940; Raymond in January and Laura in November of 1942; Nathaniel in 1944; I was born in 1945; Jimmy in 1947; Janice in 1948; Ronald in 1949, and pretty little Doris in 1951. Glenn Arthur died at seven in 1947 in a drowning accident and Nathaniel (Nat) died following a 1975 bar accident when he was thirty.

Having eight brothers and sisters was sometimes great. We had to depend on each other every day because often there was no one else to take care of us. We did a lot of things together to take care of ourselves, especially after my mother eventually left. And as bad as some of his actions seemed, Dad did a lot to take care of us as well. Dependency was key and trust was essential among us. At times, especially after Momma left, we had to hunt for food or beg for it from stores in places like Salinas, Hanford, and Huron because Dad would leave us to look for her. I recall going into a store in Salinas and asking the owner for bones for our dog. But we took the bones, picked some carrots and onions and made a stew for ourselves.

Nathaniel was my favorite brother. We were just eleven months apart. If my second-grade teacher had not held me back, we would have been a lot closer as we grew older. As children, though, we really had a great time in spite of our hardships. Nat was about the same height as me, but he was much thinner. I was always heavy-set like my father. Nat was a lady's man, even as a young boy. The girls fell in love with him while I just hung around, hoping to catch any rebounds. As we grew older, he maintained his charming ways.

Nat seemed to be my alter ego, but we were polar opposites. I believe at times he wished he were me, and I know at times I wished I were him. At other times, I felt sorry for him because he really wanted to do well, but it never seemed to happen for him. Nat just didn't know how to make a better life for himself. I tried to help him, but it was always in vain. He died in 1975, as he was descending the stairs in a bar-room and fell, hitting his head on the concrete floor. He was taken to the hospital, but the medical staff, learning he had been picked up at a bar, assumed he had just passed out from drinking and didn't properly examine him. He bled to death in the hospital. During this time, no one in the family knew where Nat was, or someone might have been there to help him. The next morning when the doctor arrived it was too late. The hardest decision we ever had to make was to give permission to take him off of life support. But Nat would have wanted it that way. Surviving on a machine was not his style. After all, he was a lady's man, and he had a reputation to uphold, but I still miss him even now.

Some of my most precious memories involve my broth-ers and sisters. There was the time my grandfather, Jimmy Johnson, took us out to either pick fruit or cut wood, I don't recall exactly which. It was extremely hot that day and we had not taken any water with us. My grandfather had a jug of wine, which he allowed us to drink. When we returned to my grandmother's house we were all drunk. My mother was beyond irate, because we were stumbling and falling all over the place.

Then there was the time that Thomas shot himself in the foot with his .22 rifle, and the time he built a raft and all the brothers got on it and pushed off into the deep just before it sank. None of us knew how to swim, so Thomas, the ship builder, had to play lifeguard and save us all.

There was also the time when Nat told my sister Janice to touch a hot electrical wire. Of course, neither of them understood the dangers of a strong jolt of such a current, but the whole ordeal turned out to be pretty funny. As Janice held onto Nat, she grabbed the wire, and the shock had poor Nat shaking like a flag flapping in the wind.

Hanging around Nat was always an adventure, like the time when he was bitten after he put his hand into a hole in the ground trying to retrieve a squirrel. On another occasion, Nat and I were walking home through the projects in Paso Robles when he spotted a very pretty girl. I yelled at him to watch out, but so blinded was Nat by this young beauty that he didn't respond soon enough. When he finally turned to see what I wanted, he walked into the light pole head-first and knocked himself out cold.

Life during these times was very hard, but with my brothers the days were full of laughter. For example, there was the time when we were walking in the country and spotted a cigar box in the middle of the road. We all decided to race for it, but Raymond was the fastest. He reached the box first, grabbed it and held it high as he continued running down the road. Suddenly, we heard a loud yelp as the box went one way and Raymond another way. We ran to see what made him disappear so fast and discovered a dead rattlesnake in the box! Raymond thought it was still alive. Besides having a great laugh on Raymond, we learned a valuable lesson about picking up things without first kicking them to inspect them. To this day Raymond is deathly afraid of snakes.

When I was in the second grade, some of the fifth-grade and sixth-grade boys, including Raymond, thought it would be a great joke to turn a tiny car that was owned by one of the teachers over on its side, which they did. All the kids were yelling, screaming, and laughing. Once they put it on its side, they set it upright again. We thought this was so funny. Perhaps I was not aware of it, but I don't remember any negative consequences that came about as a result of this act.

One night while Dad was driving us to another farm, we hit a deer in the road and were at a loss as to what to do, but then we realized we had just killed our dinner. We boys got out of the car, helped carve up the deer, and continued on our way, stopping only long enough to get ice to keep the meat cold. We ate well from that deer for about two weeks.

Dad became a foreman or field boss at one of the camps. He was the man in control and everyone there worked for him. We were doing pretty well. We had a big two- or three-bedroom house, which we were allowed to live in until the picking season was over. One day Momma stepped out after having just cooked dinner, and Jimmy and I began playing with matches, setting fire to the peeling wallpaper. We'd light one piece with fire and put it out and then we set another piece on fire and put it out. Eventually, we started a fire that we couldn't put out, and it blazed out of control. I told Jimmy to get the kids while I went to get Momma.

I ran to her shouting, "Momma, you know that house we're living in, it's burning." She panicked, screaming as she ran toward the blaze. Then we saw Jimmy coming toward us with our sisters, Doris and Janice, and our brother Ronald. Momma never told Dad how the house caught fire because he would have killed us had he known. We lost all the family's personal effects in that blaze, as the house burned completely to the ground, but everyone was safe.

It was a big mystery to me and my brothers as to why Dad never capitalized on the amazing musical talent he had passed on to his sons. Our ability to sing and dance, and our talent for capturing a song after only one or two hearings was, I am sure, all inherited from his gene pool. We always sang in the car, with Nat leading while the rest of us harmonized. How, with his love of music, did Dad miss this opportunity? Clearly, there was something in his past that kept him from taking advantage of his and his sons' talents, just as there was something in him that kept his past hidden from us.

The fact that he never excelled at his own heartfelt dream of being in entertainment may have prevented him from encouraging his sons to explore the talent he had passed on to us. He started out as a singer in Los Angeles, but I can only assume that his love of bourbon and other liquid spirits may have cost him that dream, and even his soul.

But if there was one thing my father loved more than singing it was money. Still, it didn't take much imagination to realize that the potential of earning a living with our voices far outstripped any potential we could have realized by picking fruits and vegetables in the heat and dust of the Central Valley. He had been a professional singer once, so he knew that our talent could be put to better use than just singing in bars to cover his drinking tab.

People would tell him that he had a great voice and he would say things like, "You should hear my boys." Maybe he did see the potential riches we could bring him, but his focus remained limited to making just enough money to survive. All we really needed was for him to train us, and we could have made enough to not only survive, but to truly live. Our talents were ripe for exploitation, especially after my mother left and he was burdened with the care of all nine children by himself. It's funny how Dad never missed an opportunity to scrounge little scraps of money, but fumbled the huge opportunity to cash in on the talent of his sons.

As we grew older, most of my siblings thought I was weird. And they were probably right, for I always felt that I was different from them. My nickname was "the dreamer," just like Joseph in the Bible. But I did not want them to hate me or believe I was different. I never really wanted to be different; I just wanted to be loved.

I wanted to be like everyone else, though something would not allow me to do what some of my brothers would end up doing. In spite of the fun times, I had a very difficult time as a child, teenager, and young adult. I wanted to fit in with my older brothers, but the activities and pursuits they were wasting their lives on were of no interest to me. Of course, I came to realize that I was not supposed to be like them. I was different and my journey was going to be different. My brothers took the fast lane, fueled by alcohol, drugs, and the night life. They wasted their time and energies in pimping and fighting, but today two of my brothers are trying to pick up the pieces of their lives.

Another thing that was a mystery to me concerning my brothers was that they were talented singers, but they didn't use this gift. Why would they not take advantage of their talent instead of becoming pimps, winos, and drug addicts? I never understood it, except to think they wanted the easy life. But the life they chose was filled with extreme hardships. I thank God that He allowed me to be an example that they could observe in order to help them turn their lives around. I loved them and really enjoyed being around them, and still do today. I thank God every day that He spared their lives and that they are not spending time in some prison.

As for my sisters, Laura, Janice and Doris, they grew into beautiful women, wives, mothers, and grandmothers.

They all graduated from high school and got married. To-day, they are successful in their own right. Most of their children have graduated from high school and some have graduated from college and gone on to achieve successful lives of their own. I believe I am a part of that success in that I was the first to graduate from college, and thereby I set and example for them.

5

HARD LABOR

There were not many white families living in the migrant camps in the 1950s. There were white men and women who worked in the fields, but they lived mostly in the towns, not in the camps. The first time I saw large numbers of white families working the crops was when we were in towns like Marysville and Yuba City, picking peaches, and in Portersville, where we picked oranges. As we traveled north into Santa Rosa, Napa, Ukiah, Eureka, Crescent City, and into Oregon and Washington, we would see quite a few white families working in the fields. But it was nothing like the Depression/Dust-Bowl era when masses of whites migrated from such places as Oklahoma, Missouri, Texas, and Arkansas to find work in the gloriously productive fields of California's Central Valley.

One of the few white men who lived in the camps was one of my father's best drinking buddies. We called him Mr. Farb. Mr. Farb claimed he was a Harvard graduate and had taken up drinking after his wife left him for another man. I am not sure if that was true, but he seemed to be a brilliant mathematician when he was sober. Sometimes Mr. Farb would travel with us, and I would pepper him with questions about books and various subjects he seemed knowledgeable about. He would always encourage me to study hard and stay in school, which is exactly what I longed to do.

My father's other best friend was Lightnin', a black man Dad had so nicknamed because he was very dark-skinned. Lightnin' also traveled with us at times. He was always telling jokes and would play nursemaid to us kids if Dad was not around. One day when Dad was sober he cleaned our cabin and cooked beans with ham hocks. He told us to eat, but to leave him most of the ham hocks, and that's what we did. Lightnin' came over and, in spite of the warning, he ate all the ham hocks! When Dad came home, we told him what Lightnin' had done. Dad grabbed Thomas's .22 and went looking for Lightnin'. When he found him, he shot at him three times. We did not see Lightnin' for about three months. One day we were outside playing and noticed Lightnin' peeking around the corner. He asked if our father was home. Dad spotted him and told him to get himself in the house. Not being sure what would happen between them, we peeked through the window and saw them laughing about the incident. I am quite sure they got drunk that night.

As migrant farm workers, we picked all sorts of produce, as well as cotton. "If it grows in California, I probably picked it," I often tell people. We moved around, following the crops and traveling as far north as Washington. But most of our time was spent in California. We worked the small towns between Bakersfield to the south and Marysville and Yuba City to the north. We also worked in areas along El Camino Real, which is what Highway 101 is called, and other places such as Oxnard, Santa Barbara, Paso Robles, Salinas, Gilroy, San Jose, and Santa Rosa.

We spent most of our time in migrant labor camps during the harvesting season. These camps had no roads—everything was dirt. All the bathrooms were outdoors, and they were always filthy, smelly, and unsanitary.

Momma and Dad always had water around, or there were rivers and streams in which we would wash our hands and sometimes bathe. They always made us wash when we could. Maybe that is the reason none of us got any major illnesses. However, Nat, Raymond and I did get pneumonia one year when we lived in Riverdale. I was so weak from the illness that I could not even walk. My condition became so dire that they rushed me to the hospital in critical condition; I had a temperature of 105! After arriving at the Fresno County Hospital, the doctors placed me in a tub of ice to get my temperature down quickly to keep me from going into convulsions. The doctor told my mother that if I had not been brought in that night, I probably would have died the next day.

I spent two weeks in the hospital. When the doctor visited me and asked how I was doing, I told him that I was fine except for another little boy that cried all night and kept me awake. He told the nurse that I needed a quiet space and to place me in a room by myself. To a perpetually hungry kid the best thing about my hospital stay was the food I got three times a day. That frequency of decent hot food was a very rare luxury for me. My brothers and sisters came to see me, but they could not come in. I waved to them from my hospital window. Momma and Dad visited me every day and, surprisingly, they remained sober during this time.

After briefly living well in the hospital, it was back to the hard life in the camps, but during this period I did spend some time in school.

Some of the cabins we lived in had wood rather than dirt floors, with a stove in the middle, and a few filthy mattresses that could be placed around the floor. There would usually be shelves for canned goods and other items, and a small table with only a couple of chairs, so most of the time the kids would eat sitting on the floor. The wash bins for cleaning clothes, like the bathrooms, were outdoors. Sometimes Momma would use the stove inside the cabin for cooking, but often much of the cooking was done outside because the little stove could not hold a lot when you were cooking for eleven people.

We lived in camps in Huron, Five Points, Tulare, Salinas, Hanford, Lemoore, Firebaugh, Mendota, and Riverdale; those are the ones I can remember. If we were to stay the night in any of these small towns, we usually pitched a tent in an already-picked orchard or under a big tree if no other housing was available. Most of the labor camps were along the roadside, usually a few miles from the town. Each row of cabins had dirt roads in front of them, and it was our constant prayer that it wouldn't rain, because when it did the roads would turn into a muddy mess, and they would remain that way until the sun would dry them out again.

The cabins were placed directly in front of each other so that when their front doors were opened you could look from one cabin straight through the other. People usually parked their cars on the side of their cabins, opposite the wash basin that sometimes would be on the cabin wall.

Each cabin had its own water faucet and usually enough room between them for a clothes line, or an area to make a small fire for cooking or a barbecue. If there was no water basin next to the cabin, we would use a communal water basin. Around this communal water basin families would gut their freshly caught fish, or skin their recently caught rabbits, or pluck feathers from newly killed chickens. Their bounty would be cooked on a spit or grill nearby.

To understand what migrant camp life was like, there are three movies that provide us with a pretty good depiction—"The Grapes of Wrath," "La Bamba," and "Come See the Paradise."

"The Grapes of Wrath" was the fictional account of the Joad family, desperately poor whites who had lost their farm to the Dust Bowl in Oklahoma during the Depression and came west to California to seek a better life. John Ford directed the 1940 film that proved to be as brilliant as the 1939 novel by John Steinbeck.

"La Bamba," the 1987 film, was based on the life of Ritchie Valens, a teen-age rocker who was killed, along with musical icons Buddy Holly and the Big Bopper, in a plane crash in 1959. The movie was titled after his famous hit song. Valens, a Mexican-American whose real name was Ricardo Valenzuela, had lived for a time with his mother and half-brother as a migrant worker before his musical gifts came to light.

In "Come See the Paradise," the lead character, Jack McGurn, falls in love with a Japanese girl. When her father finds out, he forbids McGurn to see his daughter again. The couple runs away to Seattle, where they have a daughter. During World War II, McGurn is drafted but his wife and daughter are rounded up with others of Japanese ancestry and sent to internment camps around the country. His wife and daughter are sent to Manzanar in California's bleak Owens Valley.

The camps in these movies offer fine representations of the kind of camps we lived in as farm laborers. Oddly enough, my family, along with hundreds of other farm workers, lived in some of the camps where Japanese citizens had been interned during World War II. It was because these facilities happened to be close to the fields where we were working. However, none of the films I just mentioned depicted the migrant life from a black perspective.

Most migrant camps had a community room or cabin for social gatherings. The rooms usually had a jukebox and, often, a pool table, and a table with chairs for the men to use for playing cards, dominoes, checkers, or other games. Sometimes these areas turned deadly at night due to drinking, loud arguments and fights, including stabbings and shootings. The loud music from the jukeboxes often kept us kids awake late into the night.

The owners of the camps were the farmers, and the field bosses managed the camps. All who lived on a particular labor camp worked for the field boss. Others who lived elsewhere and wanted to work the fields arrived early in the morning to caravan to the field where we were to work that day. There were quotas on the number of field hands working a field, so most of the time you had to know the field boss and make a reservation to work with him on a particular field. It was sometimes difficult to just show up and work. However, we managed to pull it off quite a few times.

Those seeking work would usually meet at a farmer's home or ranch to get permission to work on his farm. Sometimes you could just show up at a field and hope they needed workers for that day, but you couldn't do that at many of the fields. Dad had to let the field boss know the number and names of those in our family who were eligible to work. I don't know if they asked our ages, but Dad would tell them he had six family members who were eligible to work, and all of them were very good workers. Of course, he neglected to

28

tell them that some were under age and shouldn't have been working. Laura usually would baby-sit with the younger children, but sometimes she would work with the baby nearby in a crate or sitting on a cotton sack. One time we stopped at a small farm and Dad persuaded the owner to let us pick all his cotton rather than hire more workers. The job took us only about a week, and then we were off to find other work.

The field boss would be paid by the owner of the farm, and he would pay his crew from the monies he earned. If it was a weekly payroll, he kept a book with the names of each worker in it and listed how much they picked for the day. At the end of the day or week, the figures were tallied and the workers were paid according to what was in his little book. For example, each time you brought your cotton sack to the scale the weight was recorded in the book next to your name so that you could be paid at the end of the week. If the paymaster was there, sometimes you were paid at the weight station immediately. Many of the field bosses were honest, but not all of them. You were generally at their mercy for your correct pay.

I saw a lot of ugly things happen at the fields. Mexican immigrants were often misused and abused; some were never given an accurate accounting of what they earned. I watched as some were arrested, spied on, and sometimes murdered because they were non-citizens and the authorities did not aggressively protect them. I watched as buses would haul them away under guard after they had worked a number of days. Then another bus would arrive with another load of Mexicans. I guessed that the tour of the previous laborers had come to an end and they had to be replaced. But this seemed to always happen around the time when they should have been paid. I always wondered if they got their money.

When I asked my father who these people were, he told me they were called "wetbacks" and had come to work the fields because there weren't enough people in the United States who would work the fields. The term *wetback* sounded strange to me, so I inquired further. He told me the term originated in Texas, where Mexicans often entered the country illegally by swimming across the Rio Grande River. The term would eventually apply to all migrant workers from Mexico, both legal and illegal. My father said the reason they were treated so poorly was because they didn't have the same rights we enjoyed. I never liked the term *wetbacks* and I never used it, but I heard it used by others all the time.

In the 1950s a lot of Mexican children worked the fields, just as we did. During that period, migrant laborers from Mexico were families, not just men. But in the 1960s the state and the counties began enforcing the child-labor laws. Today, it's mostly men doing the work, while the women remain with the children in Mexico.

After watching for a while, I figured out how the field bosses would con certain people out of their money. One way was to cheat them on their time sheets and the weight of their pickings, which was usually the way they conned the elderly. A second way was through the general store, which the field bosses controlled. The prices of items in these stores were sometimes triple the cost of the same items at stores in town. Running a tab for food or liquor in the camp general store was virtually like handing over your pay to the field boss, since these purchases allowed him to steal back much of what he'd paid out in wages.

Like the sharecropper system in the South, many of the poor workers, winos and vagrants, after a while were working for nothing because they owed all their money—and their souls—to the company store. Because of this, Dad made sure we never bought anything at the labor camp. Since we usually had a car, we shopped in town.

As migrants, we always carried our own kerosene stove, water, tent with poles and stakes, blankets, flashlights, cotton sacks, and other items with us in case we had to set up living quarters somewhere. What did not fit in the trunk, we carried on top of the car. For a while, we pulled a small, two-wheel trailer in which we loaded most of these items. Sometimes when we arrived at the work site, the camp would be full, so we had to set up our tent. If it rained, we were really in trouble because of the mud, which made going to the bathrooms a real adventure. Gas stations often discouraged us from using their facilities by posting signs that read, "Restrooms not for migrant workers."

However, for us kids, a greater concern with the camp restrooms was the threat of being molested by someone who might be waiting to take advantage of the situation. We never allowed our sisters to go to the restroom alone. The boys would always accompany them and stand by the door and walk them back to the cabin or tent, but it was also dangerous for younger boys who were unaccompanied. We learned as kids how to survive. Some fathers were as untrustworthy as strangers. You saw and heard of kids molested by their fathers, and I knew of girls who were impregnated and even prostituted by their fathers, all for the sake of money. It was necessary for us to take precautions, so, as kids, we never allowed anything to happen to any of us. We did what was necessary and stuck together as a family.

Working in the fields presented other dangers as well: there were snakes, coyotes, poisonous spiders, rats, nests of wasps and bees, and lots of sick, stray dogs on the prowl.

You also had to be careful of what and how you ate. Because workers tended to use the bathrooms wherever they could, it was never safe to just grab a piece of picked fruit to eat without washing it off first.

I started working in the cotton fields when I was five or six, and by the time I was seven, I had a quota of picking 100 pounds a day. Now, I really had a problem with cotton. I hated picking it because it was a tough, bloody, all-day job. Before you could pick the cotton, the boll had to be completely dry. You had to pluck the cotton from the open boll; its burrs were so sharp that our hands were a bloody mess after a day of picking. And because we had to bend over to pick the cotton, we could hardly straighten our backs in order to walk upright afterwards. In fact, some people picked while on their knees to avoid the back pain.

If you were right-handed, you put the long cotton sack on your right side and picked from the row to your right. You did just the opposite if you were left-handed. After you filled your sack you put it over your shoulder and carried it to the scale, which could be more than a hundred yards away. After getting the cotton weighed, you had to carry it up a ladder and walk a large plank to empty it into a trailer. Then you went back and picked more. It was very hard work, and workers sometimes employed any device they could to get an advantage, like putting rocks in the sack to make them weigh more.

I often thought of the black slaves and wondered how they survived the arduous work day after day and the fact that they received nothing for it. We only made three dollars for every hundred pounds we picked. Since I rarely picked my hundred-pound quota, I usually made between two dollars and fifty cents to two dollars and seventy-five cents a day. A workday usually lasted twelve hours, or from dawn to dusk, because we started work before dawn and did not finish until dusk. Sometimes we were so exhausted after work that we bypassed dinner and simply collapsed in exhaustion on the floor to sleep.

There were other crops I did not mind picking, like cantaloupes, oranges, apples, grapes, string beans, corn, plums, nectarines, strawberries, pears, watermelons, and all other melons and potatoes. I especially liked picking potatoes because it made me feel like a big kid. I had to bend over and put potatoes that a tractor had unearthed into a sack that I had between my legs and stand them up for someone to come by and tie. These sacks usually weighed fifty to seventy pounds, and for a seven- or eight-year-old to do this really was proof to my father that I was not lazy. I kept up with my brothers and would complete just as much as they had in a day. I remember Dad telling me after a day's work that he was really proud of my work efforts.

All monies earned for the day, no matter how much or how little, were given to Dad. He would give us a small amount if we asked, but he was in control of all of it. He gave us quotas we had to meet each day and if we did not meet those quotas, we were given a pretty good scolding. But Lord help you if he felt you were lazy. Then you got a spanking. Although I rarely made my hundred-pound quota, my brother Nat was picking two hundred pounds of cotton a day when he was only eight years old!

We usually started our day before daybreak at about 5:30 in the morning, which meant we had to get up around 4:30, and work until noon. Then we would have a break. After that, we would work from about 1:00 p.m.

until 8:00 p.m., or dusk. We often worked seven days a week. However, sometimes we would have Sundays off.

I sometimes got in trouble because I daydreamed a lot while I worked, almost always envisioning a more normal existence far away from the labor camps. We were a singing family, so we often sang in the fields to make the work go faster. Dad would start us off and we would back him up. We sang what today is known as rhythm and blues. We would sing everywhere—in the car, in the fields, in the cabin—wherever we went. We loved songs like "I Got a Woman" by Ray Charles, "Tweedlee Dee" by LaVern Baker, "Since I Met You Baby" by Ivory Joe Hunter (my favorite song of all time), and "Fever" by Little Willie John.

We sang songs by the Platters, Ink Spots, Muddy Waters, and Etta James. We sang songs by the Drifters with Clyde McPhatter, like "Money Honey," and later, "Honey Love." We sang "Adorable," which the Drifters recorded after McPhatter left, as well as McPhatter's "Treasure of Love."

A Louisiana singer named Lloyd Price had a few songs we loved, like "Lawdy Miss Clawdy," and "Just Because," which was another favorite of mine.

My father's favorite singers were Joe Williams, Arthur Prysock, Nat King Cole, and Billy Eckstine. Because of my mother's love of country-and-western tunes, we would sing songs like Hank Williams' "Your Cheatin' Heart."

Our biggest influence in gospel music was Sam Cooke and the Soul Stirrers. We sang most of their songs, including "Just a Little Talk With Jesus," "Touch the Hem of His Garment," "Jesus Gave Me Water," and "The Last Mile of the Way."

The only time we made money singing was when my father was in a bar and ran out of drinking money. Then he would come and get us to sing so that he could continue drinking. Sometimes we boys would sing and dance for the soldiers when he worked at Camp Roberts. Beyond that, Dad never seemed to appreciate the talent of his five sons, and I think it had much to do with his mystery past. It seemed he could not let anyone know who he really was. If his sons became famous, he would be found out. But he knew we had talent, and so did my mother who, until she left, tried to encourage us.

Singing made the work go faster. I loved it, but I was bothered when I had to work and would see other kids doing the typical kid things. Before the sun came up, we were cooking breakfast and then we would head straight to the farm-labor bus or follow it to the fields and work. We stopped in many different places, sometimes good places but most of the time bad places.

When my father worked at Camp Roberts we lived off the base in the city of San Miguel. Camp Roberts was huge, and during the early 1950s it had become a major training site for troops headed to Korea because the terrain resembled that of Korea. The Army officially closed Camp Roberts in 1970, but parts of it are still in use today by the California National Guard and a few Army Reserve units.

The nearby town of San Miguel had grown up around the historic San Miguel Mission. The city had just one theater, and there were a number of bars to accommodate the soldiers. I remember going to the theater late one evening to watch Charlton Heston, Betty Hutton, and Cornel Wilde in "The Greatest Show on Earth." It would be one of the few places where we could indulge in such entertaining activities as movie-going.

Often people in the community were less than friendly to black kids. We had quite a few fights with white kids, and these were usually very dangerous rock fights in which we would throw rocks at other kids at a distance of sixty or seventy yards away. I remember hitting a kid in the eye with a rock and being very upset with myself and wondering if he was badly hurt. I hated fighting, but usually these fights were nothing we couldn't handle since there were six of us brothers.

We also played with several of the white kids. For fun, we would go to the dumping grounds on the base, where we would find old skeletons of guns. Then we would sneak up the hill to watch the soldiers firing live ammo at the targets. After that, we usually ended up playing our own war games with the gun skeletons we could get through the fence, or racing bikes down the hills in San Miguel.

My brakes failed once as I roared downhill toward the town's main intersection. I flew right through the town with my heart in my throat, all the while thanking God that I met no cars as I went by. In spite of such dangers, these were fun times, but they were rare because most of our time at the base was spent shining shoes, dancing for the soldiers, or doing other jobs to make money.

Nat and I were walking home late one night from Camp Roberts after the buses had stopped running. We had been shining shoes and dancing, and it was about one o'clock in the morning. I was about seven and Nat was eight. We never felt that it was a problem to be walking home late, because no one ever bothered us. This time, though, we noticed car headlights and then saw the flashing red lights of a Highway Patrol car. The patrolman pulled over, got out, and asked what we were doing out so late. We explained that we were working at the base. He asked if our father knew where we were. "No," we said, "he told us to be home by nine-thirty."

The officer had us get in the car and took us home. The ride was great because we were very tired. We gave Dad the money we had earned and—purely for the benefit of the officer who was still standing there—Dad gave us a scolding. Then we were sent to bed. As I grew older, I would think of San Miguel often and realize that I really loved that little town.

From there, we moved to Paso Robles, a much larger city with lots of hills and fields to play in. We went to the movie theaters there also, and the annual rodeo was always fun. As kids, we would go for long, leisurely walks along the railroad tracks. Things seemed to be going very well for us as a family since Dad had steady work; our home was comfortable, even though it was in the projects. At that time, Momma and Dad seemed to be getting along fine.

We lived in an area where most of the blacks lived, and Dad worked for the Sanitation District. He always brought home lots of books and toys that people had thrown away. The school I attended was small and the teacher was very strict. This is where I first experienced racial prejudice from an adult, my second-grade teacher. A fellow student hurled a racial slur at me and my teacher agreed with him! She told me I should feel proud to have an opportunity to attend school with white children. I was more confused than hurt by her remarks. When I mentioned the incident to my father, he became very angry that a teacher would agree with a student that had used the n-word in addressing his son. He demanded that the teacher apologize both to me and to him. After that I was fine.

While living in Paso Robles, Momma made sure we attended church every Sunday we could. The church bus would pick us up and take us to Sunday school. I was still very much the dreamer, and I tried to understand why this world existed, what my role was in it, and what God's purpose for my life was. Also, I was still trying to figure out if our God was the same God that white people worshiped. Because we attended an all-black church, I wondered if our God was black. But why would there be two Gods? If that were so, then there would have to be an Asian God, a Mexican God, and so forth. I concluded that there was only one God, and I didn't think He was prejudiced. Still, I wondered if He helped people down here on Earth.

Because I loved to read, Sunday school was an opportune time to get some very interesting reading done, especially in the Old Testament. The New Testament was not as fascinating to me. I was taken with stories about Joseph and his coat of many colors, as well as Moses, Solomon, Ruth, Daniel, and David. Old Testament characters were very real and exciting to me. Their stories always helped me with my internal conflicts.

One Sunday I was feeling very low and sad. I think it started the night before as a result of my parents and their problems. Dad had been drinking and he and Momma had been in one of their weekly fights. Once I was seated on the church bus, I kept staring out the window, watching the new homes that were being built in and around Paso Robles. The bus was full of children who were yelling and screaming, but I was deep in thought about my future, even though I was only seven years old. I tried to lose myself in the green hills and beautiful valleys. I wanted so much to have a happy childhood, but I wasn't having one. I thought about all the children who were going to live in those new homes and about how blessed they were. My heart ached to know what it would feel like to live in one of those homes.

After Sunday school the younger children would usually be sent to another room until the main service was over. However, on this particular Sunday I felt I needed something more. A voice kept telling me to go inside the church and listen to the minister. I asked my Sunday school teacher if I could hear the sermon instead of staying in the classroom with the rest of the kids. She took me inside to join the congregation. I felt a sense of comfort, as if everything would be okay. I can't remember what the minister looked like, but I can remember his words, because they were words I was supposed to hear that day. The minister spoke of the goodness of God and how He would do anything for us, if we only believed in Him. He said, "Just ask and you will receive; seek and you shall find; knock and the door will be opened." Those words struck a chord in me and the minister seemed to be talking exclusively to me. It was as if God had come down and implanted this truth into my soul so that I would never forget it. At that moment I knew God was speaking directly to me and that was the reason He called me into the church.

"Whatever you desire, just ask in faith and it will be given to you," the minister said. "God will remove all the obstacles to ensure you receive it. Just ask in faith."

As with those ancient heroes I had read about in the Old Testament, on that day God revealed Himself to me and showed me His grace and goodness. On the ride home, I was deep in thought; I kept hearing the minister's words over and over in my head—"Ask in faith." I never told anyone about that day because I did not think they would believe me. Even if they did, I did not think they would have understood what I had to say. So I asked God to help me and my family, especially my parents.

My faith is what fueled me when I was growing up, and it continues to do so today, but religion was never important to me. As kids, we would go to church every now and then. Ministers would come out to the farm-labor camps on Sundays and preach, and then we would give them our money, which I never understood. I would ask, "Why don't they come out and help us instead of coming out on Sundays to preach and take our money, seeing how hard it is to earn?" We didn't have much money, so I never understood why we would give it away.

So it was not so much about religion for me as it was about my faith and how it led me to an unwavering trust in God, knowing that I would benefit by believing in Him. I envied white kids because they had what I longed for—nice homes, two parents that loved each other, and educational opportunities. I wanted that for my family and God seemed to be the only person who could get it for me. So I put all my faith in Him.

6

MOVING ALONG

After Paso Robles, we drifted from town to town. I cannot remember every town, but I know they were all in the Central Valley. From Los Angeles to the border of Oregon and Washington, California's Central Valley was one of the most beautiful places in the United States during the 1950s. The fields provided a living for many people whose only skills were picking potatoes, watermelons, cantaloupes, peaches, cotton, grapes, peppers, corn, beans, and other crops.

Because of Dad's strong work habits, we usually secured work throughout the year. I believe if Dad had only controlled his drinking, he would have created a fine future for himself and his family far beyond what we derived from the labor camps. Along with his remarkable work habits were his great sense of humor and a winning personality. And the money we made together as a family was often pretty good.

I could pick close to a hundred pounds of cotton, Nat and Raymond could pick about 200 pounds each. Thomas, the oldest, would pick more than 300, but Dad could pick about 500, even after drinking all night. When we pooled our money, we often had thirty dollars or more, which was a goodly sum for a household in those days. But by morning, every dollar of it would be gone, flushed down Dad's gullet in a stream of liquor.

Dad always found work. I never saw him sitting around wishing he had a job. No matter where we went or what town we were in, Dad would drop us off and when he came back to get us he would have a job. Dad was never drunk at work. He might have a beer at lunch, but he would never get drunk when he was working.

However, a big problem was his inability to stay in one place for any length of time. Although we moved whenever the crops changed or all the picking was done in one area, sometimes we moved just because Dad wanted to move. When we lived in San Miguel, he came home one night and announced that we were moving to Paso Robles.

"Why, Dad?" I asked.

"Because we're moving," was his terse answer.

He always acted as if someone was looking for him. And, considering some of his illegal stunts, there very well might have been.

Our path was from Paso Robles to Salinas, San Jose, Dinuba, Raisin City, Fresno, Madera, Chowchilla, Los Banos, Stockton, Sacramento, Marysville, Yuba City and Bakersfield, then back to Huron for the fall, during which we were in school and usually stayed through the spring. During the fall and winter we worked the towns close to Huron, such as Five Points, Hanford, Tulare, Riverdale, Coalinga and San Joaquin, which are in or near Fresno County.

Huron was a tiny town with no industry other than farming. The farms were mostly devoted to the production of lettuce, onions, tomatoes, cantaloupes, cotton, and cattle, so it followed that most of the people who lived there worked in the fields. There were plenty of bars and small stores to handle the crowds after the long workdays. My father and mother were frequent visitors to a couple of the bars. Huron would later develop a reputation as a very violent town, but I'm pretty sure my parents weren't around at the time to contribute to it.

I remember a time when we were sitting in the car for at least eight hours after working all day. We were hungry, waiting for Dad to come out of one of the bars, expecting that he would get us some food. Thomas, who was sixteen at the time, went to the store to get milk for the baby and a few cold cuts for the rest of us. Finally, we went into the bar and found Dad passed out from drinking. My brothers and I had to carry him to the car, and Thomas had to drive us home. We had not eaten except for the cold cuts, and we would not eat until the next day. This was something Dad did fairly frequently. He would go into a saloon and drink and leave us waiting in the car for hours, sometimes during the heat of the day.

One evening after Dad had been drinking and was inebriated two police officers pulled him over. They told him to get out of the car and made him walk a straight line. Then he had to touch the tip of his nose with his index fingers. Amazingly, he passed both tests. One of the officers pointed a flashlight into the car. We were all piled in the back. The officer asked Dad if we were his kids, and he said, "Yes."

"Hurry home and put those kids to bed," the officer told him. I watched the whole incident, and to this day I cannot explain how my father passed those tests.

At other times, after a day's work Dad would drop us off at the camp and leave. Sometimes he would come back that same evening, but at other times he would be gone for a week or more. Looking back, it amazes me as to how I made it out of that kind of life, but then I remembered the minister's word, so I kept holding on to my faith in God.

I can remember at least four labor camps in which we lived and worked around the Huron area. At one, my father was the contractor or field boss. Two others were Camp 28 and Camp 29, which were about ninety-nine percent Mexican. We were given temporary lodging at Camp 29 once, but were continually harassed by the Mexican kids who believed that blacks shouldn't be there. Walker's Camp was black, and we were at Camp 29 only because Walker's Camp had no cabins available. It was run by Mr. Walker and his two sons and a daughter. The camp was located about ten miles north of Huron and about five miles from a little town called Five Points, which had five roads that intersected in the middle.

We had been in Walker's Camp many times, and it played a particular role in our lives. It is the camp where Momma finally left us for good, and it is where our grandmother from Fairmead and our uncle from Los Angeles would come first if they wanted to find us. It is also the camp where my godmother, Madonna, came when she tried to take me back with her to Los Angeles. It is also where a friend of my mother's came to visit with her husband or boyfriend, and got into a fight with him in their car after taking us to the store for candy. He stabbed her in the leg with an ice pick while I was sitting next to her in the front seat. I jumped out of the car while it was still moving, not injuring myself, but I was very frightened. Dad was so upset; I thought he was going to kill someone.

We had friends at Walker's Camp and played many kid games there when we were not working. I was still a loner in school and at home, but I did play with some of the kids in the labor camp. In fact, my brother Thomas eventually married Merdis Smith, a woman from Walker's Camp.

Because our mother had left and Dad was usually not around, Merdis' mother would cook us biscuits some mornings. She would often make more than she needed for her own family, so we would go to her cabin, get the biscuits and take them to our cabin for breakfast. Sometimes Thomas would go out and kill a rabbit, come back and skin it, and cook it for our breakfast. Because Merdis' mother was able to get welfare assistance, she would give us cases of beef and gravy they had received from the county welfare office. The food saved our lives, because we had nothing to eat while Dad was gone. I remember having beef and gravy, powdered eggs and powdered milk for breakfast, lunch, and dinner, with homemade biscuits every now and then. I still have fond memories of Mrs. Smith and those biscuits.

I only remember two families from Walker's Camp, the Smiths and the Byrds. Both were large families. The Smiths settled in Stockton and the Byrds followed us to Fresno. Their families stayed intact, but ours didn't. Thomas married into the Smith family and Raymond and Nat stayed in contact with the Byrds.

Janice, Jimmy, and I made friends with some white kids who lived across the street from Walker's Camp. We picked cantaloupes for their father. They would invite us over to watch television. This could have been the first time we had seen television. However, it is possible that we might have seen television earlier at my uncle's house. I am not sure about this, because when we would visit my uncle in Los Angeles, my aunt would usually make us stay outside on the front porch until my father returned to pick us up. She would not allow us in the house!

Sometimes perfect strangers will treat you better than your own relatives.

7

MY FATHER'S FOLLIES

Momma had a history of leaving every now and then after a fight, but she would usually be gone only for a few days and then return. Finally, after a fight at Walker's Camp, she apparently gave up on the marriage. We hadn't seen her in about week. We asked Dad about her, but in the back of my mind I feared she might be dead, and that maybe Dad had killed her. He simply told us that she had left and wasn't coming back. He was right. She didn't come back.

We found out later that she had run off with a man named Bill. They had settled far away in Arizona because they were afraid my father would find them. I wouldn't see her again for about four years. She left nine children behind, the oldest of which was about sixteen and the youngest was four.

It wasn't only the fighting and drinking that got to her. She told us later that if they had continued fighting, either she was going to kill my father or he was going to kill her. We were fortunate in that there was no gun in the house at that time—Thomas had left with his .22 and gone to live with our grandmother—but there were knives around. Momma stabbed Dad at least once that I know of, and maybe twice during their time together. He responded by beating her with whatever he could find. She knew they were getting to the point where someone was going to be killed, so I believe that is why she left. I was eight years old, and I did not see her again until I was twelve.

One time earlier, as we were traveling through the mountains on our way to Klamath Falls, Oregon, Dad and Momma got into a big drunken argument. Since I always sat in the front seat between them, I was caught in a violent verbal crossfire, with all their venom gusting over my seven-year-old head. Finally, Dad got so angry that he stopped the car and told Momma to get out. "I'm going to kill you if you don't get out of the car," he said. So she got out and slammed the door with such force it felt as if our eardrums would burst. All of us were startled senseless by what was going on and fearful of what might happen to Momma on the road by herself. But when we got to our destination, Momma was there. She had caught a Greyhound bus and beat us to Klamath Falls.

What did they fight over? Everything and nothing—other women, the lack of money, but most of the time none of us knew what their fights were about. Often, Dad would come home late, or he would go off and leave her somewhere. Sometimes he would leave her at a bar, forcing her to find her way home alone.

When Dad wanted a drink he thought nothing of putting his kids at risk. After arriving in Klamath Falls to work in the string bean fields, Dad drove off on a side road and eventually stopped at a little shack out in a field. The window panes had long since been broken out and the roof was half gone. The shack probably had never had lights and gas, and there were no signs that anyone had lived in it for many years. Still, Dad dropped us off with a few blankets and a flashlight and left. As the sunlight sunk into the darkness, he still had not returned. In fact, it was not entirely clear to us that he knew where he'd left us. We huddled together in this one-room shack full of big rats that raced through the place freely, literally jumping over our feet. We had no choice but to take turns staying awake and using a flashlight and a stick to keep the rats away from the others as they slept.

In the morning when Dad hadn't returned, my brothers and I left the girls and walked to the town to look for him. We found him passed out in his car. These kinds of stunts that Dad pulled regularly tormented me. I never understood how he could neglect us in such careless ways.

We worked in Oregon for a while and then drove up to Washington to pick apples. Then we returned to Marysville on our way back to Huron and picked up Thomas, who had spent some time with our grandmother after having a big fight with Dad.

We encountered other dangers that Dad had nothing to do with. During peach season in the 1950s, the cities of Marysville and Yuba City were overrun with migrants who were seeking work in the orchards. Most families had no living accommodations, so they turned the riverbed into a community and most of us lived in our cars under the bridge. Because the evenings were so warm, those sleeping in cars kept the windows rolled down to escape the heat, but most people built makeshift tents attached to their cars and slept on blankets under the tents. Both of these scenarios were scary because bats constantly flew under the bridge. Occasionally they flew into the cars and the tents, which was horrifying because bats are hideous creatures that resemble flying mice. So we would pass the night fighting off the bats, which seemed to be everywhere.

Because it was hot and we were cramped, most of the family slept outside on the ground, except for my sister Doris, who was a baby at the time; she slept in the car. We made sure she was protected from the bats or whatever else that might be considered harmful.

At one point Dad befriended a couple in the town. My father always had a way with people, and his personality was such that others were drawn to him. It is said of some people that they never meet a stranger, and this was certainly true of Dad. However, this naïve couple asked Dad to watch their home while they went on vacation. But a funny thing happened to their home while they were away: Dad sold it and we moved back to Huron.

As mentioned, with Dad, we were notorious for robbing the local winos. I don't think we ever seriously hurt anyone physically, though we certainly bruised a few drunken egos. I'm not trying to justify our actions at all; we did it at Dad's direction.

We also stole from stores. My father was one of the best shoplifters around. He was so gifted at it that shopkeepers would look at him and never guess that he had enough stolen food on him to feed a large family.

And being the hustler he was, he also drove cars that he never paid for. Using my grandmother's address, Dad talked a salesman into giving him a two-year-old 1951 Buick in exchange for a small down payment. After driving off, Dad decided he didn't like the green color. He went back and exchanged the green Buick for a black one, but he never made another payment! His modus operandi was to simply make a small down payment, leave town, and not return until the next year. He always seemed to get cars, and if he had trouble with them, he fixed them himself.

Usually when the fights started up between Momma and Dad I would become so angry that I would go outside to sit on the porch or just be alone. Often I would just take a book and begin to read, to put myself in another place. I would be angry with them, angry with life, angry with people, and angry with God. I did not understand why we had to live in such an unsatisfactory way with our parents drinking every day, staying out late, and sometimes not even feeding us. If my father started to drink, my mother followed suit. She never took a stand and said, "I'm taking my kids and going home to get them some food." She resented the idea that she might miss all the fun while he stayed in the bar. Her attitude was if he was going to drink, then she was going to drink. It sometimes seemed as if no one cared about us kids. So I started to ask questions like, "What did I do wrong?" "Why was I brought into the world to go through this?"

I felt it wasn't fair. If God was supposed to be fair, then why was He treating us unfairly? I thought that I must have done something to anger Him. What I longed for was the kind of stability that families I read about had—the kind of stability some of the families I saw while working on the labor camps had. I would watch families that had nice homes with picket fences, and there we were—living in migrant-labor camps, in one-room shacks or sometimes even sleeping in our car. Meanwhile, my mother and father would drink up every cent we had labored to make, with no regard to how their behavior was affecting their children. We were working in the fields like slaves and truly living like slaves.

As a child, I wondered about the universe and where we all came from. I used to lie out in the orchards at night looking up at the sky and wondering what was up there beyond the stars. One Christmas Eve, my brothers and I claimed we saw Santa Claus and his reindeer flying through the sky and knew we would not get any Christmas gifts because we did not have a house with a chimney, so we wished that Santa would just drop some gifts to us as we watched him go by.

I also believed God favored white people, because they seemed to be the only people who were being blessed. I remember reading books on the discovery of America and how people would pray before they left Europe and pray again when they arrived here. So reading these books on America and how white people seemed to prosper, even during slavery, always bothered me. I firmly believed that God had to be white. Every image I saw depicted Jesus as a white man. I thought, "They are white, so He must be fine with what they are doing to enslave black people, because He is God, the Creator of the universe." I felt if He was not happy or satisfied with their actions, He would do something about them. Since He didn't, I felt He somehow approved of their actions.

But I remember asking myself, "Where was the God of black people?" Is He the same God that white people have? I would think that if He is God of all the people, then He must have cherished white people more than black people, because they seemed to be getting more blessings than black people were. I questioned the act of going to church and praying to a God who was not listening. Still, I told myself that maybe He would listen to a child, regardless of his race, because surely God would not hurt a child.

I started questioning why I couldn't have been white and why I couldn't live like white people. As I look back, I realize now that the answer as to why I was born into the world under a particular set of circumstances was not for me to know. But I do believe God's plan for my life would not have been fulfilled had I not been through all the hardships I was forced to endure.

Remember, I was a child who was trying to understand my family's circumstances at that time. But as I matured, I put away this childish way of thinking and held onto the belief that everything that happens, good or bad, was part of God's greater plan for our lives. Most people did not understand me, especially with regard to how I could allow such deep thoughts to put me into a dream-like state. Most adults would just shake their heads and whisper, "That boy is strange." One time Dad asked me what my problem was since I hadn't responded to his calls when he was only about a hundred feet away. I told him that I did not hear him. He asked what I was I doing. "I am thinking," was my reply. He asked, "What about?" I told him I didn't know. He responded by saying that since I didn't know what I was thinking, I should just think myself down that cotton row and get to work. I couldn't say anything else but, "Yes, sir."

I had learned the skill of tuning things out, a technique I frequently employed because of my family's large size. There would be so many of us packed in the car and making so much noise that I trained myself to tune out the others and concentrate on what I was reading, or the clouds outside, or just a thought. I would later use this method in church to eventually read the Bible three times through while the service was going on. Pity someone who called to me, because I surely would not hear them.

I watched my parents grow old quickly, their aging sped up no doubt by the heavy consumption of liquor and the constant bickering. Watching the drinking and smoking take total control of a person, especially one's own parents, can be very difficult on a child. I know it was for me.

Today, I am totally turned off by drunks. I guess that is why I cannot sleep while riding in a car, bus, train, or even when I am flying in an airplane. The thought of leaving someone who is inebriated in control of my life is frightening to me. In his drunken stupor, my father would often get behind the wheel and take off wildly with all of us in the car. I would be so afraid that he would have an accident that I would force myself to stay awake to talk to him.

Today, when people talk about secondhand smoke, I think about all the long rides we took as small kids with the windows rolled up while Dad smoked his way through three packs of cigarettes! It's amazing that none of us developed asthma or any other respiratory problems.

When my parents were sober they sometimes made sure we had food first, and then they would go off and enjoy their booze. It seems to me that most of the adults around us in the camps fed their children cheap food and themselves cheap booze. This was the norm—hard work, rowdy music, cheap food, and hard liquor. My dad would drink any type of alcohol, but his liquor of choice was whiskey. Momma drank mostly beer and wine.

I witnessed firsthand how some poor people were turned into alcoholics and drug addicts. These were the only outlets for their state of mental bondage and low self-esteem. Five of my brothers would follow in those footsteps and live similar lives of dread and despair. All five of them became either drunks, drug addicts, or both. Later, I almost succumbed to this cycle myself because I saw no way out. I started drinking socially in the military and continued after I got out, but I always had a job or attended school. I never stopped trying to improve my life. Still, I came home drunk one too many times and thought to myself, "Hey, wait! I'm drinking too much!" So I quit. I thought about my parents, and my brothers and I said to myself, "I'm not going that way."

The more I read and the more I observed life, the more I became convinced that society did not care about poor black people, or their children. My parents never had a chance. They never *lived* in American society; they only *existed* in it, nibbling around the edges of real life. Even today I hurt for them when I think about those wasteful times. There was no master plan to place such people into a system where they could make a real contribution. And, like Black Wall Street in Tulsa, when enterprising blacks did work together to pool their abilities, their capital, and their genius, whites always found a justification to storm in and destroy what blacks had built. My parents were still slaves and the Emancipation Proclamation never became a reality during their lives.

Why would a society not try to ensure that all its citizens, in spite of the color of their skin, participate to their full potential? I have always wondered at what age my parents came to understand that they would never get a chance for a good job or never be treated with respect and dignity in their own country. Deep down, I wondered how they really felt. Years later I would often wonder how I would have clothed and fed nine children and a wife without an education, without true freedom, and hardly any help from the government. I could see it was taking a toll on my parents. There were fights, hard drinking, adultery, and many nights of sleeping in our car under bridges, or in tents and old houses, and filthy farm labor camps.

Today I wonder how many millions of people our society has let go to waste. What a different world we would have if all that talent were used to its fullest potential. It is sad to see the waste of that talent along with the other things on our planet that are abused and not allowed to thrive and prosper as God intended.

My parents, Thomas (Curly) and Alberta, circa 1950s

*My elder brother,
Thomas, circa 1958*

*Thomas's first
wife Merdis*

My *favorite picture of* Mattie (top)

Mattie and me, circa 1970 (right)

Mom and Dad Gamble, my in-laws
(bottom)

Mattie and me (right)

Daughters Diona, Angela and Anna, plus me and Mattie (middle)

Daughters Angela, Anna, Diona and Natalie (from my first marriage)—and me (bottom)

Me at Randolph Air Force Base (top)

Me at 19 (above)

Me at Roading Park in Fresno (left)

Nat and girlfriend
Ruby, circa 1966

Raymond, circa
1965 (below)

My brother
Ronald at my
wedding, in
1970, standing
between my two
best friends,
Milton Ray and
Bruce Smith
(far right top)

Mattie and me
with my sister,
Laura, and
her husband,
Robert Taylor
(far right bottom)

Doris and her husband,
Steve (top)

Laura and husband,
Robert (left)

Janice and Thomas
(below)

62

*My brother, Jimmy
(above)*

*Thomas and my
sister-in-law, Patsy
Clay (left)*

63

Sisters-in-law, Tammie, Loretta and Schelia, with my sister, Doris (2nd from left) and former brother-in-law Joe (circa 1970s) (top)

Janice, Nat and Jimmy (right)

My sisters Laura, Janice and Doris (below)

64

My sister, Janice, and her husband, Robert Armstrong

Me, five of my grandchildren, plus a little friend on the far left.

8

SCHOOL OR BUST

During our labor camp days we were rarely in school on a regular basis. School was of secondary importance to my family at certain times, but on occasion we were able to attend. My dad would enroll us, but because we were constantly on the move, he would pull us out, sometimes after only one day. As migrants, we usually did not stay in one place very long. Especially during the summer and fall months, when the most time we would spend in one place was usually a week or two. However, during the winter months, when there was not much harvesting going on, we would stay for longer periods, sometimes as long as six months. But school was not the highest priority for our parents.

My first memory of school was the first grade in Fairmead, but I attended about twenty different grammar schools between the first and third grades. The Fairmead school was approximately two miles from where we lived. But I had such a difficult time in school in the first and second grades! It wasn't that I wasn't capable, but by that time I had already attended roughly ten schools and was having a difficult time adjusting to the constantly changing school environments and new kids. And I was extremely shy. I would fight anyone who said a word to me, especially the girls. I cried if the teacher asked me questions in front of the other kids.

One day my mother got a note from a teacher that told her that I was missing too much school. For that I got the whipping of my life. Although I did not miss a lot of school after that, I continued to have problems participating, so much so that when we had our school play, I was given the role of Little Boy Blue because the role required me to do nothing more than lie in the hay.

I had to repeat the second grade because the teacher said I was too shy and would not participate in class. She determined that I was not mature enough to go on. Though I was crushed at the time, I would later come to realize that repeating the second grade was one of the best things that happened to me, because it helped me to find my place by putting distance between me and my older brothers, Nat and Raymond, who were headed down a wrong path. Raymond was a wild one and a big influence on Nat. Nat, on the other hand, was a big influence on me. Repeating the second grade caused a separation that allowed me to develop at my own pace. Later, they would be out running the streets, but I was not a part of their circle anymore and they no longer wanted me hanging around them.

Still, having to repeat a grade wounded my fragile self-image and caused me a great deal of despondency. I felt dumb because none of my older brothers and sisters had ever repeated a grade. I became obsessed with studying, and I told myself that they were smarter, so I had to study harder than they studied to prove that I was just as capable as they were. I would never be held back again, I told myself. I became terrified of even getting a "C" because I felt such a grade was not good enough to keep me from being held back. I experienced no relief from this form of academic terror until my senior year in high school. In fact, from the third to the eighth grade I would always ask my teachers whether or not I was doing well enough to move to the next grade. Of course, during those years my older brothers would tease me cruelly about being held back, and they constantly reminded me that I was not only the dumbest, but the darkest and ugliest of the Hill children, and I had the biggest nose!

When we lived at Camp Roberts I went to school regularly. The hills around San Miguel were full of sheepherders. I would often go up into the hills above the city to watch them herd their sheep, and I spent hours talking with them about sheepherding. In fact, I frequently ditched school to spend the day with them. Since I was a loner and considered strange or different, I also wanted to know what it was like to live their type of life, alone with no one to communicate with but the sheep. The greatest lesson I learned from them was that it was okay to be by myself. However, they encouraged me to use the time wisely in order to read, think, and dream. I was already a great dreamer.

My only saving grace while working as a migrant was the opportunity to read. I read on the way to the fields or at lunch. Sometimes I would sit down in the fields to read. When Dad stopped at a bar I had plenty of time to read. I am not sure how I learned to read as well as I did with all the relocating, but while the other kids were out playing I would read. Reading became my outlet when I needed to shut out my surroundings. I read everything from books to newspapers and magazines. Reading proved to be the only consistent thing in my life. Books had a way of sustaining me, giving me hope of a better life, a life beyond the cotton fields, vineyards, and orchards. When I would get lonely, I would read and daydream. Often I was transported into the life of a character in the book I was reading.

I read such works as *The Adventures of Tom Sawyer*, *The Adventures of Huckleberry Finn*, *Black Beauty*, *National Velvet*, and even comic books like *Superman* and others. But it was often hard to find books at the camps.

After reading a book on Abraham Lincoln I asked my father if he knew that Abraham Lincoln was raised in a log cabin. He said he did. I asked how Lincoln could rise from such humble beginnings to become the sixteenth president of the United States. If he lived the way I'm living then I can do the same, I reasoned. "I'm going from a migrant labor camp to the White House," I told my dad. "I'm going to do what Abraham Lincoln did." My father gave me the strangest look.

I loved reading about Davy Crockett and presidents Andrew Jackson and Thomas Jefferson. I never got into thinking that I couldn't do things because I was black until I became a teenager and began reading about all the things that were done to limit black people, especially in the South. The thing with me was competition. It never dawned on me that people would try to stop me.

I started to collect books, and there were people in the labor camps who bought them for me. One elderly couple took a special interest in me. I would go to their cabin for dinner and to read. When they decided to move and rented a house in Fresno, they asked my father if they could take me with them in order to give me a better chance of getting an education. They told my father that I was a gifted child who should get an education. My father refused, questioning why everyone was trying to take his son from him. Earlier, my godmother had tried to take me with her as well, but my father had refused to let me go.

I knew I was one of my father's favorites, along with Nat, Janice and Doris. I closely favored him in looks. Dad was nicknamed Curly and he called me "Little Curly." No one ever called him Thomas, his given name. I think he always wanted me with him. He thought I was special. I could say things to him that others couldn't and he would accept them. He never wanted me to be disappointed in him, even though I was, and I think that bothered him.

Sometimes he would take me with him on trips to visit friends at other labor camps. Looking back, I think my father knew I was going to make it out of the labor camps and to college, and he wanted to be there when I did. I had resolved at an early age that I would not be a farm laborer all my life, and now I had the extra burden of proving that I was not dumb and that I was going to graduate from high school. All I ever wanted was a real chance at life. I began to pray to God for my chance. After nothing happened, at least not on my timetable, I decided to take matters into my own hands. I dredged up the courage to ask my father if I could attend school every day and work nights and weekends. He said no, because all the other kids were working, so I should do the same. Being out of school was not in my plans. If I did not attend regularly, it was a cinch that I would be held back another grade, and I could not let that happen again. I had to attend school full-time.

I began to get up early and leave the cabin under the pretext of having to go to the restroom to relieve myself, but I would hide in the field until after the farm labor bus had left. Then I would come out of hiding and wait for the school bus to pick me up. But the offer by the elderly couple may have influenced my dad's thinking. Not long after that he finally agreed to allow me to attend school full-time. He knew he was not going to stop me from getting an education because people were telling me that I had the ability and to keep reading because the only way out of the fields was through education. Dad was afraid of losing me, so he allowed me to go to school in order to keep me with him. I was more than delighted, but I soon realized that the road to answered prayer was not always paved with gold.

One of the grammar schools I attended was in Huron. I could feel that the other kids did not want to play with me or sit next to me on the bus because of the way I smelled. My mother was gone, and sometimes I didn't bathe for long periods of time. My clothes were ragged and unclean, and I would have to wear the same clothes and shoes with no soles on the bottom.

I was beyond being embarrassed. I would ask the teacher if I could sit in the back of the class by myself, because I did not want to disturb the other kids with my body odor or have them make funny faces at me or laugh at me. She allowed me to sit in the corner, and when recess came, I would ask to remain in the classroom to read a book, clean the blackboard, or do anything other than go out and play. Often I would just sit there and cry, thinking how unfair my life was. But at other times the teacher would take me by the hand and lead me outside and make me play. I did not want to play because I had ragged clothes, no soles on my shoes, and I knew that the other kids were going to make fun of me. I was especially self-conscious around the girls.

One thing people seemed to agree on concerning me was that I was smart, so I decided that one thing I could control was to keep up with the other kids as far as doing my homework and studying. I decided that no matter what grades they got, I was going to get the same grades or better. I was not going to be the dumb kid in class with torn clothes, no soles on his shoes, not getting his class work done, and not being able to read and do math. I understood there were some very well-off kids in the school, but that did not mean they were smarter than me. To have them even think that way would upset me. I just wanted to prove to my teacher and my classmates I was a capable student.

I would do my schoolwork at the cabin on the dirt floor and sometimes under the headlights of my father's car, if he wanted the lights off inside the house. But I always turned in my homework. Sometimes it had dirt and crud on it, but it was turned in the next day. My behavior instilled in me that I was just as good as kids who may have had more than I did. They may have had both parents at home with no alcohol or drugs in the home, but I applied myself and determined that I would get the same grades they did. This new outlook on life made me feel good about myself, at least in that respect, although I still had to battle feelings of low self-esteem.

Miss Nancy, my third-grade teacher at Huron Elementary School, was my favorite of all time. She was and still is a hero to me. It did not matter to Miss Nancy that I had not bathed or brushed my teeth or used deodorant. She saw something in me and made sure I was included in the class discussions. She would come over to my desk and show me how to work a problem or correct a sentence. I would be embarrassed, because I knew I did not have a pleasant smell, but this never seemed to bother her. She would smile at me and pat my head and say I was doing a good job, and this would put me on cloud nine. She would encourage me by holding my hand and praising my work.

Even though I think it was her first teaching job, Miss Nancy showed great compassion and an understanding of my circumstances. Perhaps she was aware of other students in similar situations and guessed that I did not have a mother at home. She certainly would have known that most mothers would never send their child to school looking the way I did, not having bathed or having been properly groomed, and wearing the same clothes every day. She was my teacher from September, 1954, to March, 1955, but she is the reason why I challenged my father to let me go to school. I wanted to see her every day.

Most schools, especially schools with farm labor camps nearby, provided free breakfasts for poor children, but I was too proud to get my free breakfast. Miss Nancy noticed this, and instead of asking me in front of the class if I wanted breakfast, she would give the class an assignment and take me by the hand, walk me to the cafeteria, wait for me to eat, then walk me back to class to save me from the humiliation of having to ask to go, or deny that I really wanted to go, or do without a proper breakfast. Miss Nancy was a great lady, and I will never forget her and what she did for me. She really made me see that school was a place where all students should enjoy the same comfort and respect as any other kids, regardless of their situation.

My being poor and living in a migrant labor camp meant nothing to her. I would not be allowed to use that as an excuse for not getting my homework or reading my assignments. To Miss Nancy, poor students in her class would be treated the same as the other students, and she expected the same quality of work out of them. I never thought anyone would treat me as an equal with white kids, especially if they were white themselves.

Because of Miss Nancy's kind treatment, I developed a healthy love and respect for teachers. They were people I trusted and strove to please. If my teacher liked me and treated me with respect, I had a great time in school. If my teacher showed disrespect toward me or was upset with me, or if I thought I did not please my teacher, I sometimes would go home and cry. I never wanted to upset my teachers. Later in life I began to figure out why this was so. I began to realize that my teachers became my mother, father, sister, and brother, because they showed a great interest in my work and would give me the encouragement I craved. The desire to please my family was transferred to my teachers.

Any time we went to a school we would take the books and store them in the car. After reading my own books, I would read my older brothers' and older sister's books. In those days when you were a new student, the schools gave you the tools you needed most—books, paper, and pencils. We would take these supplies and put them in the trunk of the car as we moved from one place to the next. During these trips, I would practice my reading and writing. Early on, when I read the book, *Fun With Dick and Jane* (and their dog Spot), I visualized their family's home with a white picket fence in their white neighborhood, and I wondered if my family could have lived in Dick and Jane's neighborhood.

Because of my reading, my love of school spiked upward in the third grade. I had knowledge and insight that was different from most kids my age. I had read about the Constitution, the Bill of Rights, and the history of the United States. I had read stories about George Washington, Abraham Lincoln, and how the country was founded and settled. I had read books on Daniel Boone, Davy Crockett, and Kit Carson, and how the West was won, all from the white perspective, but never the Native American's. I read about the Alamo and how Davy Crockett and Jim Bowie lost their lives trying to save Texas from Mexico.

I began playing a game when I read a book. I visualized all the characters as being black, because I wanted to see myself and other blacks living as the people in the books lived. I did not want to live in a farm labor camp or in the projects with alcoholic parents. Having read Tom Sawyer and Huck Finn, I dreamed of going on an adventure by myself. I was very tired of my life and I longed for something different. A great deal of my time was spent daydreaming, even while I was working, but my father would catch me and tell me to stop looking at the sky and get to work. I believe he thought I was lazy. However, I was just bored with field work and wanted something different.

From Miss Nancy in Huron all the way through high school, I usually tried to work to the fullest of my ability. There was rarely a problem with teachers not treating me with respect. I recall high school teachers telling me that education was the key that would open life's doors. You are smart enough, they would tell me, to get a college degree. I remember telling some of my teachers I wanted to be a doctor, and not one of them ever told me that I could not accomplish that goal, if I applied myself.

Most of my high school classmates thought I would become a professional singer, but they did not understand my fear of failure. I believe that is why I did not pursue a singing career. Not having ever developed a lot of confidence, I was just too afraid of rejection.

9

THE VISITOR

I called upon the Lord in distress: the Lord answered me, and set me in a large place...

Thou has thrust sore at me that I might fall: but the Lord helped me.

The Lord is my strength and song, and is become my salvation.

–Psalm 118:5, 13-14

Around the summer of 1954 I became very despondent. At this time, Momma had been gone between six months and a year. I cannot remember the exact day she left, but it was at least earlier that year. I do remember everyone missing her. How she lived such a life with Dad for as long as she did amazes me still. Theirs were down-and-dirty-drag-out fights, with knives, bottles, sticks, and stones, which were used as weapons of their warfare. We often made wagers on who would win. Dad was almost six feet tall and outweighed her by about sixty pounds, so you can imagine that he won most of the fights. Though she was only about five feet, three inches tall, you could not count Momma out automatically, because she could usually handle herself pretty well.

Their fights were often so brutal that afterwards both would usually need a doctor's care. One time Dad brought home a bull's horn that was made of clay. During a fight, he hit Momma over the head with it, and we thought she was dead. She was taken to the hospital and needed several stitches to close the gash in her head. Fights like these were commonplace, and we all knew that if they stayed together, one of them would kill the other. Often I would ask God why we had to live that way and why He had not answered my prayers to help them.

Most of the white children I would see lived in nice homes, had new clothes, and were raised by both parents. I may have had both parents for a part of my first eight years, but I certainly did not have a nice, stable home environment or new clothes.

I was especially glum, tired of living as a poor kid in a farm labor camp with no future, and getting food from the Smith family to survive. I did not understand what I had done to God to deserve this. I could not understand how He made the decision to place me with parents who would drink, fight, and do everything except take care of their children, but I was determined to find out why.

I don't want anyone to think I did not love my parents, but I was tired of their lifestyle. I was a child who would not show his feelings, especially if I thought it would hurt another person. My brothers and sisters never knew how I felt because I would never discuss my feelings with anyone. When I struggled with a problem, I would go off by myself. I was very despondent and upset, and when I got into such a mood I would go to the back of the farm labor camp where people discarded their old cars, a place where kids at the camp would play. I wanted to be alone with my thoughts.

I still carry that behavior with me today. I was always talking to God about my life and asking Him to help me and just to give me a chance. I had begun to have doubts about God. It seemed as if He was not listening to me, and I was not getting any answers to my prayers. I was extremely disheartened. I felt my life was not getting any better. Momma had left and Dad had spent months looking for her while we labored in the fields by ourselves. This had gone on for about eighteen months, which I felt was more than enough time for God to act. During this time we ate mostly canned beef and gravy for breakfast, lunch, and dinner. Although other people sometimes cooked for us, we usually took care of ourselves.

One late fall evening, when I was feeling particularly frustrated and sad, I began to think no one cared about me anymore. So I decided to run away to Los Angeles to see my godmother. I could not have cared less about what happened to me en route. I would leave that in God's hands. If I died from starvation, got hit by a car or was murdered, that would be okay. I was focused on leaving and finding a better life. If I died, then I reasoned that that was what God intended to happen. I think I secretly longed for death so that I could talk with God face to face and ask why He determined that I should have the life I had. But for the moment, I was off to Los Angeles. The only problem was, I neither knew where my godmother lived nor her full name. I only knew that we called her Aunt Madonna, and I intended to find her.

I rose early, feeling very sorry for myself on the day I was set to leave. It seemed as though I had been praying for a long time for a chance at a better life, but no one was listening. I lowered my head and began to pray again until I noticed that I wasn't alone. I don't know how long the figure had been there, but I heard his voice. This figure was speaking with his back to me so that I could not see his face. I couldn't identify him, but I could definitely understand him, and I knew it was the voice of a male. He never turned around and I never approached him to try and see his face, but he spoke to me. I had no idea who or what he was, but I do know that someone did something to me that day that made a big difference in my life. I kept telling myself that I was going to be all right. I don't know if I saw anything that morning, maybe it was just my imagination or my inner consciousness. Whatever he was, he repeatedly asked me, "What is wrong with you?" Each time my response was, "I am tired of living like this." I tried to explain the circumstances of my life at the labor camp, my parents' fighting, my mother leaving, and my desire for a brighter future.

"You keep telling me about your environment, but what is wrong with *you*?" the figure asked. "I notice," he continued, "that you look like you have a brain, two eyes, a nose, two ears, two arms, and two legs—you seem to be a perfect specimen." He made me realize that what I was seeing as negatives were really positives. As the figure explained it, these experiences were learning experiences; they were experiences I would need in order to become a complete person as an adult.

"Look at the poor and never forget them," he said. "Look at the winos and never forget them. Look at the way people are treated and never forget. Learn from the winos, the drug addicts, and the poor; always remember the way you felt when you were here. Remember your surroundings are only the environment. Don't become your environment;

only learn from it. If you believe in a Supreme Being and trust Him, you will rise above all this."

This was the lesson I carried with me through adulthood and around which I forged my mission in life.

But the conversation was far from over.

"Now, tell me what you want," the figure demanded.

So I did. I told him I wanted to be placed in an environment where I could learn and grow. I wanted to live in a place where I could attend school full-time and not worry about working in the mornings. I tried to explain to him that my concern was not for material things and that I did not care about money or clothes. I wanted a home that was full of love and nonviolence, a place where I could be with people who cared about me and my brothers and sisters. I told him that I wanted a chance at life. If he provided these things for me, I promised that I would not let him down. My only requirement was to have my brothers and sisters with me and to eliminate any harm that could come to my parents. Though I loved my parents deeply, I just didn't want to live with them anymore.

When I looked up, the figure was gone. My first reaction was that it was a dream, despite how real it felt. At that moment, I felt that I had finally gone crazy. I sat there saying, "Okay, I'm talking to myself." For days I could not get what happened out of my head, but I knew that I had had a visitor, a spiritual being, and I talked to him. I also knew that I could never tell anyone what happened. And I never did until now.

The figure and I both made promises to each other and those promises were kept. Six months later a man who was married to a woman named Rosie caught Dad with her. Rosie's husband apparently underestimated my dad, because when he attacked, Dad beat him so badly that the man had to be hospitalized. Dad was put in jail. My father probably told the authorities that he had nine children at a migrant labor camp. Therefore, the county of Fresno sent people out to get us and take us to a foster home.

The figure had kept his promises. Now it was my turn. The figure visited me that evening and spoke with me several more times for many months. I became a totally different person during those years. I was resolved to get an education so that I could live a better life and help others do the same. None of my brothers and sisters understood why I was so focused on achieving my goals. I don't know if God came down Himself or if He sent someone else to speak with me. I don't know who that person was, but I do know that from the moment he appeared, I felt that something was going to happen to me that would change my life for the better. And it did.

Over the years, my mind has tried to discount these visits. I have told myself that they never happened. It would be more than twenty years after our marriage before I would even tell Mattie, my wife, about the visits.

Every time I tried to discount the visits I would look back on my life and ask, "What else could have made me so different?"

10

A New Beginning

Dad was in jail, Momma had abandoned us, and we were off to a foster home. On Friday, March 4, 1955, we left the farm-labor camp forever. It was the day before my tenth birthday, or so I thought. After getting into foster care, my foster mother was able to get my birth certificate, which showed that my birthday was actually March 29 rather than March 5. March 5 was my younger brother Jimmy's birthday.

When the Highway Patrol came to pick us up we ran into the bushes and hid. We knew the police had come after someone and we did not want it to be us. So the word went around Walker's Camp that the police were there for the Hill children. My older brother, Thomas, had to come round us up one by one. Thomas was sixteen and had become the head of the family after my father was taken away. They put us in one car with one police officer, and at first we just sat there and cried because we were scared. We thought we were going to jail. After all, why else would the police be there? The Highway Patrol officer tried to explain to us that we were not going to jail, only to the county office in Fresno.

The last time we had gone to a county office a woman friend of Dad's had tried to use us to swindle money from the county. I remember her telling the county staff that a man had left nine kids with her and, therefore, she was able to get lots of food and money. "I am taking care of the kids," she told them. It was all a big lie, and when my father found out what she had done he made her give him the money.

Naturally, we felt something similar was going happen again. But the officer said, "No, you are going to become wards of the county." We had no idea what he meant. As we headed into Fresno, we began marveling at some of the homes we rode past. "My God, look at these houses!" we said to one another. "Look at the way these people live! Look at this big old house here and that one over there! I hope we live there."

We were astounded at the tall buildings in downtown Fresno. This was all new to us, as we had always lived in small towns and worked in the fields; we had not been in large cities for quite a long time. Although Fresno is not a large city by our standards today, it truly was to us then. We had not been in a place with so many stoplights, so Fresno was as large as they came from our point of view. Everything was so fascinating to us.

There were all kinds of emotions running through me at this time. As we were riding, I was hoping this was the answer to my prayer. I did not tell anyone, but I was talking to myself the whole time with these words of affirmation, "I know I am going to be okay." All the fear had evaporated from me. We all knew we would be okay.

Fresno, which has always been known as an agricultural center, was a city of about 100,000 at that time. It is known as a gateway to Yosemite National Park and the Sequoia National Forest. Fresno becomes quite cold in the winter and extremely hot in the summer. It is known for the dense Tule fog that settles in the San Joaquin Valley during the winter after heavy rainfalls. The fog makes driving dangerous for long periods of time. We would get to know the Tule fog well.

It was also a segregated city; blacks and Mexicans lived on the west side of town and whites lived everywhere else. During the next ten years I would become well acquainted with the city and many of people who lived there. This was my new home and I expected to make the best of it.

After arriving in town, the Highway Patrol officer took us to a building where we met our foster mother. I can remember that moment so clearly. She came over to us and said, "My name is Mrs. Seals, and all of you are going to live with me and I am going to be your mother and take care of you. Would all of you like that?"

We all replied, "Yes, ma'am."

She would tell us later that we had such good manners, that we were the best-behaved children she had ever met, especially in light of the fact that we had come out of a migrant labor camp.

"You kids were so respectful," she would say. "It was always yes ma'am and yes sir."

I was never sure what she expected of us or why she expected anything different, but she told us she was amazed.

The question we all had now was how long we would stay with Mrs. Seals. No one told us whether it would be a week, a month, or a year. That part was very difficult for us to deal with. I hoped it would be forever. However, I told myself that when and if I left the Seals home, I would head for Los Angeles to find Aunt Madonna. But we all fell in love with Mrs. Seals immediately. She was such a kind and comfortable person. On the way home she stopped at Black's Market on California Street. We had never been in a supermarket, only in little stores in the country, and we could not believe how much food was in this market.

Mrs. Seals had a huge basket, and she filled it with food. She asked if we wanted anything special and we said no. Maybe we were too overwhelmed to say anything, so Mrs. Seals brought us the typical things you would get for kids: ice cream, candy, cookies, as well as milk, bread, cereal, and meats.

"How are you going to pay for all of this?" I asked.

Mrs. Seals told me not to worry, that she would take care of it. We could not believe she was buying so much food. We could remember going to the store and getting bread, salami, crackers and maybe some hotdogs, but nothing like what Mrs. Seals bought. After stopping at the market, we headed to our new home in Mrs. Seals' yellow 1953 Pontiac.

The funny part was that one of the houses that my brother Nat had admired as a place where he would like to live happened to be Mrs. Seals' home. To us it looked like a mansion. It was a huge yellow house with big trees in both the front and back yards. There were lots of play areas, a wading pool, a picnic area, and chicken coops full of chickens. The house was surrounded by one or two acres of undeveloped land with many different fruit trees and vines—peaches, apricots, grapes, oranges, grapefruits, almonds, and plums. There was also a building out front that had once been a restaurant. The house had four bedrooms, a living room, a family room, and a dining room. The kitchen was very large, and it had a breakfast nook. There were two long hallways that led from the bedrooms to the living room. Mrs. Seals pointed out the boys' bedrooms and the girls' bedroom. We could not believe that we had our own bedrooms that were almost the size of our cabin at the labor camp. The girls had their bedroom in the back. Because there were six boys, we had two rooms. In each room there were two full beds, so we slept two to a bed. All of our lives we had witnessed other people who lived like this and now we were among them.

We immediately felt welcomed by Mom and Pop, as they became known to us. Pop was an elderly gentleman who was about sixty-nine years old. He was a minister, and he welcomed us into his home with open arms. Rev. James Seals was born in Terrell, Texas, in April, 1886. He told us that in his youth he and his brothers had a history of drinking and fighting. He had to leave the state because he was wanted by the Texas Rangers for fighting a police officer. Pop said that his family begged him to leave town before the police killed him, as they had done to one of his brothers.

He set out for California in the early 1920s, arriving in the Golden State by wagon, and in Fresno by freight train. At that time Fresno was just a "one-horse town," as he put it. However, something good happened to him on the way because by the time he arrived in Fresno he was a born-again Christian and had accepted a call to the ministry. He built a church, Trinity Church of God in Christ, on the west side of town, at Plumas and O'Neill.

Pop had two daughters by a previous marriage. One daughter had died by the time we met him, but the other—his namesake, Jimmie—lived in Fresno and became our "big sister." Pop's best friend was a man named Lemon Peagues, who had a sister back in Louisiana who was a widow with two children. Peagues wanted her to come to California to get married. Pop generously offered to send for her and marry her if she came. Mom did come and she and Pop remained married until his death in 1979, for almost fifty years.

Velma Seals was born in Longview, Louisiana, in 1909. She was a smart child and wanted to be a doctor, a very unlikely ambition for black girls in her day. In those days African-American girls were expected to get married and have children, so that is what she did. She married a man name Fritz McMillan. Fritz was a good-looking man, but he drank a lot and beat Mom whenever he felt like it. My foster sister, Jean, was born prematurely after Mom was kicked in the stomach by Fritz, which is believed to have caused Jean's mental disability. Fritz was killed in an automobile accident while driving home drunk one night. A son, Fritz Jr., had long since married and moved away from home.

Mom and Pop built a home at 1330 W. California Avenue and began taking in foster children in the late 1930s. According to my social worker, theirs was one of the best foster homes in the history of Fresno, and they took in more than a hundred children during their foster-parent career. They told us later that the greatest gift given to them happened on March 4, 1955, when we arrived. We would remain their children until they both died. Mom passed away in 1990, the saddest day of my life.

While delivering special comments at her memorial service, I spoke of how she and Pop took in children they had never met and lovingly raised them to be responsible adults. I said that some of us had not lived up to what she and Pop taught, but we still had time to change. I told how she had inculcated a belief in God within us and had helped us understand the importance of an education and the importance of raising and teaching our children properly.

Mom was very special to me. She taught us so much about life and how to help others. She taught us that education was the key to a successful life. She valued education and wanted all of us to go to college. She preached that message every day. I remember her saying her job was to take care of the house and our job was to get an education. She was so proud that I went to college and graduated; she would talk about it all the time.

Before James and Velma Seals became Mom and Pop to us, we decided to hold a family meeting, because we were not sure what to call our new parents and we wanted us all to think the same about them. So we sat down and debated concerning what we were going to call our new mother. We decided to call her Mom Seals, but in deference to her, we asked her what she would like to be called. She asked us what we wanted to call her.

"We don't know—Mrs. Seals?" we asked.

"No, I don't want to be called Mrs. Seals," she protested. "You can call me Mom."

So we started calling her Mom. Then we decided to ask our foster dad what he wanted us to call him?

"Rev. Seals?" we asked.

"No, don't call me Rev. Seals," he said. "Just call me Pop."

So they became Mom and Pop. We also had a talk among ourselves and decided that this was a wonderful opportunity and a nice home where we wanted to stay for as long as we could. But it was at this meeting that Thomas told us he would be leaving to live with our grandmother. We all begged him to stay, but he said he was too old for parental discipline anymore, and that he would continue to visit and check on us. He returned to our grandmother in Fairmead, but soon after enlisted in the Army. He visited us whenever he was home on leave.

The rest of us made a pact that no one was going to mess this opportunity up, especially Raymond. We felt that Mom and Pop were wonderful people and that we needed to stay with them as long as possible. So we agreed that we all would behave and treat our new parents with respect and obedience. Raymond also agreed, but we knew down the road he would break his promise, because that was Raymond.

Our first night in our new home we all had to take baths, the girls first and then the boys. We could not believe that we were bathing in an actual bathtub! I could not remember if I had ever taken a bath in one before. Mom bathed both the boys and the girls, except for Raymond, Laura, Nat, and me who were old enough to bathe ourselves. Then we sat down and watched television while Mom cooked. Laura and Janice helped set the table and we ate fried chicken, mashed potatoes, gravy, green beans, and corn bread until we were full. Mom had even baked a cake for dessert. It was wonderful. The older kids washed the dishes and cleaned the kitchen. I think we talked with Mom and Pop for a long time after that about school and other things.

Mom said we would attend their church on Sunday and would start school on Monday. The school was Madison Elementary School and was not too far from where we lived. She said she would take us the first day and after that we would take the school bus that stopped in front of the house. After our talk we went to bed for the first time in our new home. Nat, Raymond, Thomas, and I slept in one room. Jimmy and Ronald would sleep in another room and Janice, Laura, and Doris shared the back room. I remember Nat, Raymond, Thomas, and me talking late into the night before we fell asleep. When we awoke the next morning Mom was already up cooking breakfast. She told us that she was going to take us shopping for school clothes that day. We could not believe that we were going to get new clothes on top of all our other blessings! I could not remember the last time I had new shoes and clothes, nor could I remember the sizes I wore.

Off to downtown Fresno we went to shop, but talk about your country bumpkins! We had never been in a downtown area and did not understand the stoplights. When the light turned green we were too frightened to cross with the cars that were moving on the green also. Mom kept telling us to walk, but still we held back. She then paused to consider her newly adopted family, and began to explain that the cars stopped on the red light, but it was okay to move with them on the green light. She told us all to hold hands and we would run across the street together, and that's how we crossed over. In many ways this was symbolic of our crossing over from the hardship and filth of the labor camps to a better life. It was a mental crossing over, a physical crossing over, and an emotional crossing over all at once. We had left our life in "Egypt" and were crossing over into our promised land with Mom and Pop. We were astonished at the richness of the soil and the size of the fruit in this new land of milk and honey. It was exactly the life I had prayed for.

A further shock awaited us as we reached the department store. We had never been in a store where you tried on your clothes before you bought them. So proud were we of our new clothing that we asked the salesman if we could keep them on and put the old ones in the bags. The salesman, quite amused, said yes. We took those old clothes home, bundled them up and put them under the bed in case we had to leave, since we had no idea how long we would be with the Seals. We were always in survival mode. We thought we might be there for a week or two. If we had to leave, we planned to take both the new and old clothes with us.

Because of our experience with missing meals, we would often take food and stash it in our rooms, usually under the beds, in case we had to leave during the night, or be without food in the mornings. When Mom became aware of it, she assured us that we would not be leaving and that there was no reason to hoard or hide food.

Mom and Pop proved to be staunch disciplinarians, and we got our fair share of spankings. You were always to say "Yes, ma'am" and "Yes, sir" to every question, never just "yes" or "no." The latter responses would bring a swift backhand to the mouth. Also, children were to be seen and not heard, especially during adult conversations. When adults started to talk, we were to get up politely and leave the room without being asked, and we were never to interrupt an adult conversation to ask a question; we waited until we were asked what it was that we wanted. And forget about asking for something more than once. If Mom said she would be with you in a minute, it didn't matter if that minute was an hour; we waited.

Mom and Pop kept us very busy with lots of chores. Pop believed that children should not be idle. We always had to keep our rooms clean, wash the dishes, and help Mom wash the clothes. Saturday was always a busy day. Because we lived in the country we raised chickens, turkeys, hogs, and a cow sometimes. We also raised our own vegetables and our own fruit (oranges, grapefruit, plums, grapes, almonds, and apricots). On Saturday mornings, we were allowed to watch cartoons and westerns, such as those starring Roy Rogers and Dale Evans. We also watched "Sky King" and any Warner Brothers cartoons that came on. During the week we never missed the "Mickey Mouse Club" (the boys had to see Annette Funicello) and "American Bandstand."

On Saturday nights we studied our Sunday school lessons for the next day and we always watched television that night as a family. I will always remember "The Perry Como Show" and how happy we were whenever a black performer would appear on television. We never missed "Amos 'n' Andy" and the 15-minute-long "The Nat King Cole Show." That is, until it was abruptly canceled after a few shows because stations in the South refused to carry it, and sponsors became afraid to advertise their products on a show that southerners didn't want.

Sunday mornings we would get up very early to get ready for church. Mom would cook breakfast and get all of us ready by 9:00 a.m. Pop usually helped the boys get dressed and Mom had to do the girls' hair. Sometimes Pop would take us to Sunday school and then return to get Mom for church. But most of the time we all rode together, the ten of us in their station wagon. Because we did not know any of the kids at church, we all sat with Mom that first Sunday and listened to Pop preach. There were quite a few kids at the church. We made some acquaintances that would become life-long friends, most notably, the Smith and Frost families.

Mom had a few rules that she would enforce at any cost. The major one concerned church attendance. We had to attend church every Sunday and any other times she and Pop felt we should attend. I remember telling myself that if I had to attend church, I was going to learn from it. I was going to be the smartest kid in the church. I was going to read everything I could about church. Once Mom and Pop learned that we could sing, Pop had us sing at the next Sunday's service. In fact, once Mom and Pop were aware of our talent, they encouraged us to keep singing, but Raymond wanted to have nothing to do with it, and Nat would eventually follow Raymond with regard to this.

I read the Bible three times from cover to cover; I studied religion from mail-order services, and I became the smartest kid at the church. I even taught the adult Sunday school class when I was twelve. When I went to Sunday school I knew the lesson, but I was bothered by the fact that none of the other kids did. I never understood why anyone would go to church and not understand why they were there. Sometimes I would ask Mom, "Why am I studying when nobody else studies?" But after a while I didn't care. During week nights I would do my schoolwork, and on Saturdays I would study my Sunday school lesson. I remember telling myself that I would do everything I could to please Mom and Pop. Whatever it was that made them happy made me happy.

Still, before I submitted to their rules about churchgoing, I had long before begun to develop my relationship with God. I would sit in the pew at Pop's church and voice silent prayers, asking God to bless everyone in Fresno, especially the poor, my classmates, my brothers and sisters, and to continue to bless me and give me wisdom so that I could be a good young person for my foster parents.

I usually prayed the same prayer each Sunday unless I knew of something special I wanted God to handle. But most of the time I was waiting on the minister to speak, so I could critique him, including Pop. The preaching was my favorite time of the Sunday service. In fact, I didn't like much of anything other than the preaching. I had become a student of the Bible, and I wasn't as interested in the singing or anything else. I always wanted to find out how much I knew about the Bible, so this was my testing time. When we lived in the squalor of the labor camps, I kept thinking that

God did not mean us to live as we were living. Now I began to feel that as blacks generally we were very religious, but we seemed to have no faith. To me, it was not about religion; it was about faith in God.

I also thought that if we believed in the same God white people believed in, then why had white people lynched so many of us? Those same people who had done the lynching called themselves Christians. I also wondered how people could lynch us and God would do nothing about it. Pop said I was going to go to hell because I asked too many questions. I told him I didn't think God wanted us to be second-class citizens. I told him I thought white people, not God, wanted us to be second-class citizens.

God said we should put no other God before Him, but my feeling was that when our people worshiped or obeyed the white man we had made the white man our God. What the white man said we couldn't do we had accepted as fact. The white man told us we couldn't vote or get an education and we accepted it. I determined that he would never get me to bow down to him as God, because his God and my God are the same God.

Later, after graduation and the military, I stopped going to church. I guess along the way church became boring to me because after I learned something I was ready to move on, not go back every week to hear the same thing. I would rather spend my time off helping people than sitting in church for two hours. When I was growing up, Sunday school was great, but I began to get bored in church services. Even though I participated in the choir, where Nat was the lead vocalist, and in Young People Willing Workers, where I became the youth leader during my high school years, I was becoming bored.

I am not sure what turned me off with church; I think it was because when I was growing up I felt most black people in Pop's church were into the idea of organized religion, but did not have the faith I had. To me it felt as if all they were waiting for was the next life, and this life was not important to live. I started to believe that they were so beaten down by poverty and white America that they had given up on this life. I decided that was not going to happen to me; I was going to live my life to the fullest. I was going to take advantage of every opportunity that was presented to me. And if no opportunities were presented, I would create them. I had, and still have, faith in one God, and I know He will take care of me.

As a young person, I tried to discuss these issues with Mom and Pop, but whenever I tried to discuss what I felt was a misuse or misunderstanding of the Bible, they would tell me to remember that I was still a child and should not be correcting adults, so I lost interest. My beliefs are rooted in my own strong faith and I think it is the faith that a person has that will get them through what they need to get through in life. Even today I have a hard time with churches, but I don't have a hard time with my own faith and what I believe. I am a true believer in Jesus and what He did for me and, like I have done most of my life, I keep my faith to myself. I know God knows how I feel.

He saved my life.

11

THE CHOSEN ONE

We started school on that first Monday after arriving at our new home. It was March 7, 1955. Madison Elementary School was deeper in the country, so we had to take the bus. Ronald and Doris were the only ones who were too young for school. Ronald was scheduled to start in September of that year. The teachers assumed that we were all slow and would not be able to keep up with the other kids. They assumed that we could not read, write, or do math. I was placed in a class of slow readers, but when Mrs. Heath, the teacher, asked me to read a paragraph, I read it perfectly. "Who taught you how to read?" she asked. I told her I had taught myself, but had learned the basics of reading and writing from the many schools I attended. I told her that I practiced reading and writing on my own when I could not attend school. She immediately placed me with a higher reading group and told me what she expected from me.

Most of the teachers took to us very quickly. I think the word had been spread among the teachers that six children were arriving from a migrant labor camp and I am sure they did not know what to expect from us. However, six children arriving at one time at Madison was a big deal, especially six black children, because there weren't many black students enrolled there in 1955. The six of us became very popular at Madison because we were friendly, athletic, and musically inclined. We all did very well, and I think Ronald was the only one who ever had to repeat a grade.

The teachers at Madison were some of the best teachers I ever had. They were tolerant, perhaps because the school was made up of a lot of poor kids from Fresno. The teachers always treated the black and Mexican-American students in the same way they treated the white students. If you were smart, they expected you to achieve. They did not expect me to get poor grades once they became aware of my abilities. It didn't matter where I came from; if my grades slipped, they would counsel me and tell me that they didn't think Mom would be proud of me for getting those types of grades.

My teachers put notes on my report cards saying that I was very smart but needed to spend more time on my homework, especially on writing. One commented, "If Johnnie would study a little harder, he could be an 'A' student because he is very bright."

My favorite class was history, but my worst was English. I would not get above a "C" in English until college. For some reason, I could not master verbs, adverbs, nouns and pronouns. I don't know why I had such a hard time with English in elementary and high school since I read all the time.

After a year or two in foster care, Mom and Pop expected a lot from me. Mom once told me that she and Pop often talked about me a great deal, about how I seemed different, how I was so inquisitive, and the fact that I read all the time and was very studious. When we arrived at Mom and Pop's I noticed all of the books they had in the living room. I asked if it was okay if I read the books and Mom said that it was as long as I put them back when I finished. I read copies of the Book of Knowledge, an annual volume that was published with updates of world news, and would read and look through all the encyclopedia volumes. I soon became interested in the evening news and would watch it with Pop. My introduction to the world of politics came during the re-election of President Dwight D. Eisenhower in 1956, as we watched him defeat Adlai Stevenson a second time.

Pop later told me I always obeyed and never caused any problems for them. However, I think my older brothers and sister had some issues that they never worked out with Mom and Pop. It could have been because Raymond and Laura were thirteen when we arrived at our foster home. They were accustomed to living somewhat on their own terms and making most of their own decisions. Momma had been gone for some time and the eldest was Thomas, who had joined the Army. Raymond and Laura felt they were rightfully the next in line to head the family and make rules for the rest of the kids. However, Mom and Pop were making the rules. We were in their home and they were the providers, so they held all the cards. I think Raymond and Laura had a problem with that, especially since Mom and Pop were not our natural parents.

Raymond and Laura rebelled in their own ways and eagerly anticipated turning eighteen so they could leave home. Nat, the next oldest, wanted to follow Raymond, just as Raymond wanted to follow Thomas, so Nat also adopted an attitude of waiting for the chance to flee. I was out to prove that home was where I wanted and needed to be. I was determined never to leave before graduating from high school. I never wanted to live with my real parents again.

Kids both at church and school teased us because we were in foster care.

"Where is your real mother?" one would ask.

"Why do you call Mrs. Seals Mom?" came another question.

"She is not your mother," said someone else.

I would always defend us and insist that Mom was our mother after all. Mom was the one who was raising, feeding, and teaching us. To me, that qualified her to be our mother. These questions bothered me at first, especially since I felt it was really no one's business outside of the family. But I did feel awkward making gifts at school for Mother's Day and Father's Day, because the gifts weren't being made for my biological parents. Such concerns bothered me for quite a while, but in time I grew past them and began focusing on me and not on my birth parents any more.

"What if Momma and Dad come and take us away?"

I had been so comfortable in Mom and Pop's home that I was taken off-guard when that thought suddenly occurred to me. This was my new life, the life I had prayed for, and the life I was promised—my promised land. I went to school every day, and when I got home Mom was there. I did my homework, talked with Pop, watched television, read, and went to bed. I didn't have to get up at 4:30 in the morning to work the fields, or hear cursing, watch my parents fight, or see people killing each other. I didn't have to sleep on dirt floors or in a tent, or take baths in a river anymore. I didn't have to deal with winos, prostitutes, or camp bosses. I could focus on living the life that I longed for.

My brothers and sisters thought I was studying hard just to be smart, but I simply did not want to repeat another grade. I was also on a mission to prove that I was just as capable as my older brothers and sister, even though I had repeated the second grade. I kept telling myself that if I ever had to leave Mom and Pop, I would be smart enough to move to the next grade based on my age, no matter how many schools I attended. I was determined to graduate from high school with classmates of my own age. But the day soon came that my fears would have to be addressed.

My mother moved to Fresno and located us in our foster home. I remember my social worker telling me, "We found your mother, and we are talking with her about you kids." I can still hear her saying, "Your mother wants you back." I talked with the social worker about my mother's attempt to take us back. I told her I did not want to go back, and asked what she was doing to make sure that all of us stayed with Mom and Pop. I told her that what we now had was a stable home with a good environment and it was where we needed to stay.

"I'm not going back with anyone," I told the social worker. "You need to relay that to my mother. I am not going with her and I will not leave here. I will never go back to that kind of environment again."

When my mother came to visit, Mom had to make me go out to the car and say hello. As for my father, he visited us only one time while I was in foster care, one time in nine years.

One day I came home from school and Mom had papers that she wanted my mother to sign so she could adopt four of us—Nat, Janice, Laura, and me. She said that the county wanted to split us up for safety reasons in case there was a disaster. The county believed that we shouldn't all be in one foster home, but rather spread out among two or more foster homes.

I remember talking with my mother the next time she came to visit. I asked her why she wanted to take us away from our foster home. In the four years she had been away

I had become quite adjusted to a decent life in a real home, with good food and wonderful foster parents.

"I straightened out my life and I want you kids back," she said.

"I'm happy for you, Momma," I said, "but you need to understand I am not going to live with you ever again."

"But I am your mother," she protested, "and I can take you back whenever I want."

"I will not be alive a month after you take me back," I said. "I am not going. So you sign the paperwork so I can stay here. If the other kids want to go back with you, that is okay with me, but not me. This is the place for me right now, but I think you should leave all of us here." I knew my siblings would have gone back, but I could have never lived that life again.

Some time later she and Mom talked and they both agreed that we should all remain with Mom and Pop, and that they should not let the county break up the family. My mother eventually agreed that she only wanted Mom to raise her children. So Mom and Pop spent a thousand dollars to put a sprinkler system in their home to counter any fire disaster, and we had to do fire drills once a month, but we stayed together. My mother would come to see us all the time, but she had not really changed. She was still drinking and doing everything else she had done before she left us.

My mother was a nice woman and I loved her and my dad very much, but I wanted them to understand that the kind of life they led wasn't for me. I was searching for something better, something more fulfilling than what they could provide. I could not put up with toiling in the fields, drunkenness, and fighting. I had tasted a better life and I was determined to hold on to it. I just wanted to live my life differently.

As I was growing up, I always felt that no one in my family really understood or liked me. I had confided in Laura during my earlier years, but during my teenage years the only person I would confide in was my sister, Janice. She was the only one who tried to understand me, but most of the time I felt alone. It was Janice who would protect me when people accused me of being gay because I had no girlfriend and did not go out on dates or to parties. They would question why I was always at home since I was a vibrant eighteen-year-old. The word on the street was that I was "queer." Janice would always defend me and explain that I was not gay and simply liked to stay home. I was usually home on Saturday nights and did not attend house parties. I went to the movies by myself and did not hang out at the park after church, as some kids did. No one knew that I was on a mission to fulfill a promise.

In fact, it was my older brothers who first accused me of being afraid of girls and therefore being queer. It started when we were younger and still in the camps. So when we played games if they needed a girl, they always made me the girl. This had a damaging effect on my psyche, so much so that I stopped playing games with Thomas, Nat, and Raymond. I refused to join in with them and would choose to read a book instead.

Once we had moved to Fresno and had begun to live with Mom and Pop, my brothers would tell girls that I was afraid of them, and they even made an attempt once to get me to fondle a girl. Instead, I ran into the house and began watching television with Mom and Pop.

So, just as I told my mother about my plan to live my life differently, I eventually told my older brothers the same thing when they tried to influence me to adapt to their lifestyle. If they did not like me the way I was, that was okay with me, I told them, but I would not follow in their footsteps. I had no desire to live the life of a pimp, a hustler, a drunkard, or just an uneducated boob.

To grow up as I did, you always had the thought in the back of your mind that you might end up like everyone else around you—poor, a ghetto-dweller with no skills and no chance for a better life. You felt almost condemned to live the same life you came from, never seeing the other side, never leaving the general area to travel or find out what the world had to offer. I wanted to see other countries and not be hemmed in on the west side of Fresno, only taking occasional trips to Reno, Las Vegas, San Francisco, and Los Angeles. I wanted out. Nor was I going to be stuck in some low-level job or settle down with some woman whose idea of fun was drinking, drugs, and partying. I had set goals for myself, and anyone who stood in the way of those goals was dismissed immediately, including the so-called saints at Pop's church. No one was going to control me and put me in a box, or try to get me to behave the way they thought I should behave. And no girl was going to trap me into marriage until I was ready.

I had a plan to leave Fresno after I graduated, and maybe head to Los Angeles where I could seek a career singing, but first I wanted to enter the Air Force and get my military commitment behind me, especially since they were offering a year of education for every year served. I would have the G.I. Bill to provide me with educational and other benefits even if I did not subsequently make it in entertainment.

I returned to Fresno years later after becoming an adult, and most people did not know I was the brother of Nat, Raymond, Ronald, Thomas, and Jimmy. They would ask why it was that no one knew me. After all, everyone knew all the other Hill brothers. But I was fine with that. I was especially fine with it once my mother reached the point of understanding me. (I lived with her for a while following my discharge from the Air Force in 1968.) She respected me and was proud to have a son who was going to college. She once told me that she hoped my brothers would one day wake up and realize that the way I had chosen was the right way to live. She conceded that Mom and Pop had done a good job with me.

Pop had become my best friend and mentor. I would confide in him and even tell him what other teens were saying about me, because I didn't follow the pattern they thought I should follow. I once asked him if I was weird or if something was wrong with me. I asked him why it was that I was not, or could not, be like my brothers. Pop told me that sometimes it seemed to him that I did not belong to the same family because of my demeanor and behavior. That comment bothered me well into adulthood, as I never wanted anyone, especially my siblings, to think I was someone special. He told me that I had been chosen, but at the time I could not comprehend what he meant. He explained that God usually chooses one person to save a family and I was that person for my family. He told me that even if I wanted to do bad things, I would not be successful at it and if I did not choose to do what God intended, I would not live very long.

"You really have no choice," he concluded.

Pop's words were sobering and I never forgot them. I always felt I was sent to Pop so he could guide and mentor me into adulthood. I believed his counsel, so much so that years later when I sought his advice about the difficulties in my first marriage, he helped with my decision to seek a divorce and marry my second wife. In fact, his advice proved invaluable when I considered marrying a young woman who was introduced to me by my sister, Doris, and her best friend, Schelia Gamble. She was Schelia's sister, Mattie.

Things went pretty smoothly after Pop explained that I was the chosen one. I loved school and had no problems advancing, but I sometimes wished I had spent more time studying and going after straight A's. I wish someone had counseled me about scholarships and preparatory courses to get into a four-year college. I really did not spend enough time on my lessons and I know I could have gotten better grades in high school. Although I made a lot of friends at Central High, I wished I had attended Edison High, which was predominantly black. The administration there cared about black students who were capable of becoming high achievers. I did not feel that Central cared enough about me achieving a higher education, so I did just enough to graduate. I played football and basketball, and ran track, but my love was music. I loved to sing and I became the lead soloist in the mixed chorus at Central.

I looked at music a little differently than many of the black kids I knew in Fresno because I enjoyed music across a wide spectrum. I loved many of the white singers, including Elvis Presley, Conway Twitty, Frankie Avalon, and Paul Anka. Some of the black kids also loved their songs, but I also bought all their records, so that set me apart. I also loved Chuck Berry, Little Richard, and Fats Domino. And I liked the Drifters, the Platters, Dion and the Belmonts, and others. In addition, I enjoyed such crooners as Frank Sinatra, Sammy Davis Jr., Perry Como, and Andy Williams, among others.

I would go to see any movies that were Rodgers-and-Hammerstein productions—"South Pacific," "Oklahoma," "Carousel," "State Fair," and "The Sound of Music," while most of my friends had never even heard of these movies. Exposing myself to a wider range of music and actually enjoying musicals added to the legend of my strangeness, but I really enjoyed music other than R & B.

By my junior year, I had become a leader on campus, especially among the black students. In those days there was a jukebox in the cafeteria, but all the artists were white. I questioned the principal about why there was no music by blacks available to us. I was told that they didn't know where to find the music of black artists, so I made up my mind to find black music for the school. I bought records for the jukeboxes. I also challenged the placement of some black students in special-education classes, and no black student was ever suspended without the principal and dean of students talking with me about the matter first. I became a champion for my people.

Because I was a good student and was looked upon as a role model, I never had any problems talking with the principal and the dean of students. Every teacher at Central respected me as a leader on campus and in the classroom. If they had a problem with a black student, the teachers would seek me out and say, "John, we have this problem. What do you think we should do about it?" I would ask them to let me talk with the student and try and resolve the issue.

Even on the bus, the driver would always listen to me if a student got out of line. One day during my senior year the bus driver was having difficulty trying to drive in a safe manner on a very foggy day. It seemed as if everyone was yelling and screaming, and the bus driver seemed very nervous. I stood up and told everyone to sit down and be quiet. Everyone sat down and became quiet and we made it safely to school.

Growing into a leader at Central High surprised me because when I first arrived at the school, the dean of students called me into his office and read me the riot act. He told me he would not accept any problems from me. Although my brother Nat was still at the school as a junior and my sister Laura was a senior, he wanted me to understand that if I caused any problems, he would kick me out. He said my brothers had been nothing but trouble and he would not accept the same behavior from me. I told him frankly, "You don't know me. I am not my brothers," and I walked out of his office. He called me into his office again just before I graduated and apologized for his remarks to me during my first year. He acknowledged that he was wrong and that I was one of the best students and leaders the school had ever had.

During high school I lettered in both basketball and football. I made many acquaintances, but very few close friends. I associated with the black, white, and Mexican-American students. Though I lived a long way from them, several white students would drive to my home to pick me up for parties or drop me off after basketball and football practice.

My best friend was Jerry Hare. He and I had been friends since the third grade. I was also a close friend of Kenneth Joe and Bill Jensen, whose parents were farmers. Bill had a sister named Sharon, who I thought was the most beautiful girl I had ever seen. She also became my good friend. Bill and Sharon were good people, and I will always remember and cherish their friendship.

As for girlfriends, I did not have one while I was in high school. There were non-black girls to whom I was attracted, but I knew I could not date them or even call them; I don't think I need to explain why. I was attracted mainly to the Latino girls and a number of them were very good friends to me, such as Dorothy Escobedo, Frances Gutierrez, Frances Amabisca, and Delores Aguilar. One of my closest female friends was Jennett Orndoff. The line between love and hate is remarkably thin, and it amazed me how such a good friendship could form from such a rocky beginning. Jennett had despised me since the third grade, but those feelings eventually dissipated around the eighth grade. During my senior year, I became very close with Divonna Johnson and Betty Skoegard, two freshmen at the time. They remained friends of mine once I joined the Air Force and afterward.

The African-American girls to whom I was attracted would never know the true desire I held for them. At that age, I did not want a steady girlfriend, but I was no fool. I liked several of them, including Betty Norman, Dorothy Johnson, Mary Warren, and Brenda Moss. I also liked May Francis Frost who attended another school and was a member of Pop's church. May Francis was the girl everyone at church thought I would marry. We were very close, but I had goals that I had set and I wanted to achieve them. May Francis went on to get married while she was in high school and I was in the military. I also had a crush on a girl who lived in another town; her name was Betty Hobbs. We would eventually marry in 1966, but we divorced in 1967. After the divorce, Pop told me to stop choosing my wife and to let God do that for me. God chose Mattie Gamble and, as always, He was right. I had attended Mattie's eighth-grade graduation since my brother Ronald was in the same ceremony. At the time it was the furthest thing from both our minds that we would marry six year later—and stay married.

But even after the marriages to Betty and my present wife, Mattie, I could never shake the fear that they might leave me for another man. Betty, of course, did leave, which put me in a state of depression for a time. In fact, I was so insecure I used to tell Mattie that she also would someday leave me. However, almost forty years and three daughters later, we are still together.

Books and movies were an obsession with me. Whenever I became depressed, I would go to see a movie or read a book. That habit is still with me today. When I was growing up, movies became a learning tree for me with regard to how to treat my parents, adults, and girls. Of course, the movies always featured white characters, but I liked the way the young people in those films had respect for their parents and their elders, and I liked the fact that girls were treated respectfully and that boys took responsibility for their behavior. I decided I would treat black girls with this same respect, but as a teenager I got a rude awakening. It seemed that many of the black girls did not want to be treated that way. I was accused of acting like a white boy. I was baffled by this, and I would later spend most of the time I had left in foster care in the company of my foster parents.

My biggest disappointment at Central involved racism and discrimination. I did not understand what I had done wrong or why I was being treated the way I was. I tried to get along with everyone and not cause problems. I did not understand prejudice and never thought anyone would treat me differently because of my race. I never disrespected the white girls, or any girl for that matter. I tried to be a perfect gentleman to them all. I just loved to sing and wanted to be a great singer, so I decided to join the school chorus. Central Chorus later formed a group in my senior year that was called The Madrigals. This group was made up of the best singers in the school. Auditions consisted of solos performed in front of the chorus. I remember practicing for days for my solo, and I nailed it. I just knew I had made the group. All of my classmates thought I had made it, too. But when the singers were chosen, I was not among them. I remember walking out of the class and calling Pop to come and pick me up. I was so disappointed that I cried. The director tried to console me and explain why I was not chosen. It was his belief that I would have difficulty getting to the recitals, but I had never missed a recital during my time in the chorus. The true reason I was not wanted in The Madrigals was because all the girl singers were white. The school was concerned about how people would react to having a black boy marching alongside a white girl. Not only was I upset about this, but all of the students in the chorus were upset as well. I had been a champion throughout my high school years. Now, my peers took it upon themselves to become champions for me and to protest the decision not to select me. The white chorus members joined in the protest, proclaiming that they had no objection to my singing alongside them.

It was always my belief that if I did everything fairly that people would treat me fairly. Yet, here I was subject to rejection based solely on my skin color. I was never the same after that. Although the director made me an alternate and I was able to sing with The Madrigals a few times after one of the regular members quit, I never quite felt as if I belonged in the group. I was even given the chance to sing "Ol' Man River" in our spring concert when we put on the musical, "Show Boat." I was still disappointed about how I had been treated, but I reluctantly accepted the challenge. I practiced for six months for my solo because I wanted it to be perfect. I was determined to show everyone that I belonged in The Madrigals. And perfect it was. I received a five-minute ovation at the end of my solo. I will never forget that moment, or the events that led up to it. That whole experience troubled me and stole a piece of my spirit and the joy I had felt in the school. I think that is when I started to have a difficult time at Central. I just wanted to graduate and leave. The way I was treated by the chorus director and my school only reinforced my resistance to putting my trust in people. With the exception of my foster parents, it seemed as though people always let me down. I had to realize, however, that it was my faith that would sustain me, and my faith was in God, not in people.

Despite the fact that I was an A/B student for the most part, I was rather disappointed with myself because I did not study hard enough to make a better life for myself upon graduation. I worked hard on my lessons and did everything I was supposed to do, but I did not have a goal except to finish high school. I did not have a sense of purpose during my senior year. There was no counselor to guide me concerning my options for college. There was no one to encourage me to apply to such schools as Harvard, Yale, the University of Southern California (USC), or UC Berkeley, and I had never been informed of the SAT. I did ponder the possibility of attending college, but I knew little about what it actually took to get into a good school.

No one at Central ever counseled me about preparing to attend a four-year institution, so I set my sights on the military. My music instructor, who was a graduate of USC, apologized to me for not steering me into music courses that would have prepared me for a major in music. He told me he was sorry because he had contacts at USC and felt certain

I would have been accepted, had I taken the right courses. I could have gone there on a music scholarship, but by the time the teacher spoke with me, it was far too late to even take the SAT. Still, I did keep my promise to the visitor when I was given the opportunity. I graduated from Central High School in June, 1964, and entered the Air Force in August of that same year.

I always think about what my life might have been like had someone instilled in me a goal-directed mind-set and had shown me how to cultivate a high level of achievement that would have made me a contender for such schools as USC. But that was not my path, and it might not have been my purpose. Either way, I felt my only option was to join the military. But I made up my mind that my life's journey would not be in vain.

Growing up poor and being in foster care gave me an insight into the problems of the underprivileged, especially underprivileged children. My experiences allowed me to understand that children who are relegated to a life of poverty suffer even more because people do not take an interest in them. God blessed me with a great foster home and great foster parents. Had I blown that opportunity to make a better life, I would have had no one to blame but myself. I knew I would not be able to blame my parents or society. The opportunity I prayed for came just as I asked, and I knew it would not come around a second time. I had once told my mother I would die if I went back to live with her. I don't know why I said it, but that statement was probably true. I don't feel I could have survived it. I may have thought that I was not ready for the opportunity I received, but I bravely faced my fears and resolved to make the most of that opportunity. That's what life is all about, taking your opportunities and doing something with them. I decided to embrace mine and discover where it would take me. I am so glad I did.

Today I thank Mom and Pop for their love and care of me from the age of nine to the day they both passed away. If I could see both of them today, I would embrace them and thank them again for saving my life. I am grateful that my biological parents had the courage to raise me for as long as they did. I believe they did the best they could with what little they had. They took care of me for as long as they could and when they could not do it any longer, they graciously stepped aside and allowed someone else to assist them. At first I internalized their absence as rejection, but eventually I understood that they had given me a chance at life.

The opportunity of a lifetime came at me so fast, and it was the promise of a better life that I had sought. It was the promise that would help me to lead and inspire. It was a promise that I will never forget and one upon which I based my life and my success.

It was the promise that I would keep.

ABOUT THE AUTHOR

I t's been decades since John Hill graduated from the struggles of a child laborer in the cotton, vegetable, and fruit fields of Central California, where he prayed to be allowed to attend school regularly. Today, he holds a bachelor's of science degree in business administration from the University of San Francisco and a master's degree in business administration from the University of Phoenix.

In 1972, he began work in private industry at Arrow Development as a payroll clerk and eventually became the personnel manager. He left Arrow Development in 1977 to work for FMC Corporation as a division manager of affirmative action before being promoted to affirmative action manager for the western United States. In 1981 he joined the Plantronics Corporation in Santa Cruz as employee relations manager, and in 1983 moved to the Rolm Corporation, first as corporate administrator and later as the Northern California area human resources manager.

He became director of the equal opportunity division for Santa Clara County in 1990. In February, 1994, he moved to the Los Angeles area and became director of the Office of Affirmative Action Compliance for Los Angeles County. In that post, he raised targets for the hiring of businesses owned by minorities and other groups identified as historically disadvantaged. He served for ten years as chief of staff for Los

Angeles County Supervisor Yvonne B. Burke of the Second Supervisorial District.

Hill is the father of four daughters. Now retired, Hill and his wife, Mattie, will soon celebrate forty years of marriage. They have seven grandchildren.